The memories of a Wobbly
are the memories of revolution
and revolutionaries. . .
of real people who filled the jails
in the free-speech fights,
and who were on the picketlines
along with their fellow workers
from coast to coast. . .
My story is their story, too.

Henry E. McGuckin

FIRST PERSON SERIES
Number Two

The author in 1970

Henry E. McGuckin

MEMOIRS
of a
WOBBLY

With an article by the author from the
International Socialist Review
(August 1914)

Afterword by
Henry McGuckin, Jr.

Chicago
Charles H. Kerr Publishing Company
1987

DEDICATION

To the memory of my wife,
at whose insistence
and with whose encouragement
I wrote it;
to my fellow workers,
living and dead,
who are a part of it;
and to the youth of today,
who are struggling so courageously
to correct the iniquities
of the past and present,
I dedicate this small book.

Henry E. McGuckin

ISBN 0-88286-157-3 paper
0-88286-158-1 cloth

LC 87-080042

Charles H. Kerr Publishing Company
Established 1886
P. O. Box 914
Chicago, Illinois 60690

Produced by 100% union labor.

INTRODUCTION

*T*his small book is written from memory. It is written entirely to remind the reader that no social changes, economic betterment, higher wages, improved working conditions, breaking down of prejudice, etc., were natural changes, but each and every one was a result of long and bitter struggle. I have written down here some recollections of my first twenty-four years at the center of activities to make possible some of the things we enjoy today. You may not agree with some of my conclusions and comments. Be that as it may. They are honest, and I came by them after seventy-five years of living close to this struggle, and in this time I have learned that an honest opinion, even if wrong, is more to be desired than acceptance of the propaganda of bigots, liberals, and turncoats who would have us believe that anyone with a contrary opinion is subversive or an agent of some foreign power. These, coupled with turncoats who have lied their fellow workers into prison and those so-called liberals whose yellow streak is a mile wide, who sell themselves for a place in the status quo, have sounded a danger signal to all who wish to maintain and advance the gains made. For as surely as the struggle to bring about these changes was bitter and long, the one shaping up to maintain and improve these gains will be even harder.

Every move to upset the applecart of the status quo is a revolution. This is true whether the attempt be in little hamlets or in the largest industrial centers. In the early 1900s, any attempt to raise wages, better conditions, or shorten hours was revolution whether it was attempted by the IWW, the AFL, or even the Brothers of Christian Endeavor. The most revolutionary organization of that time was, of course, the

IWW, the Industrial Workers of the World, the "Wobblies." The memories of a Wobbly are the memories of revolution and revolutionaries.

Much has been written about the IWW. Most that I have read has come from a very few of the top people like Bill Haywood and Ralph Chaplin, but let me make it plain there would have been no IWW if it had depended on the Haywoods and Chaplins. To build the IWW took a different kind of person than Haywood and other well-known leaders. People like John Panzner, Walter T. Nef, Vincent St. John, Albert Prashner, Jack Law, Ted Frazer, Archie Sinclair, Whitey Kline—these are real names of real people, some still living. They are a few of the unsung hundreds that filled the jails in the free-speech fights, who were on the picketlines along with their fellow workers in strikes from coast to coast. They were the ones who were beaten up, tarred and feathered. Men like Lotcham from Oklahoma. You could tar and feather a man like Lotcham, but you couldn't break him. He would be right back in the fight the next day. There were hundreds like him. I knew most of them: Lone Wolf, Casey Jones, George Speed, Tom Whitehead, Bill Chance, Jimmy Rohn, Joe Foley. . . My story is their story, too.

One

BOY ON THE ROAD

S ince these are the recollections of a Wobbly, and since it is my story as I have lived it, seen it and felt it, I have to start at the beginning, and the beginning was me. So first I must tell you who I am, where I came from, and how I got that way.

On November 10th, 17th, or 27th, 1893, I'm not sure which, I was born at Paterson, New Jersey. What happened from then until I was about six or seven is a total blank. I remember my mother's death very faintly and the funeral of the child who caused it, for her death was the result of a fall and a premature birth. Strangely, I remember the funeral of the baby but not my mother's. The reason, I think, is because there was only one carriage and a tiny little coffin which was handed in the door, and my father held it on his lap. I was left standing on the corner watching it go down the street. He was my little brother, and I never even saw him.

I remember my playmates. There were lots of them. Pratty, Tot Johnson, Murphy McCarth, Dofey were a few. I can remember the games we used to play where you would kick the can and then run half the night all over town marking the corners as you went so that the ones who were "it" could follow. I never could make sense out of it then; I can't make much out of it now. I tired of those games early, and after eight or nine I never took part in them. In fact, I began to tire of the gang and often went off by myself at night to see what I could see in some other part of town.

At the age of five I was sent to school. And although there was a public school just three blocks from our house, I was sent to a Catholic school almost a mile away. I remember thinking what a foolish thing to do, walk all that distance

7

when there was a finer, bigger school so close. One day, I must have been about eight, going on nine, I had to go to the toilet, and on returning to class I was met by one of the brothers on the stairs. He caught me by the arm and held me while he put his hand down my pants and felt my fanny. I talked with some of the other kids about this, and they told me they had been caught the same way. Well, from then on we would always be on our guard against this brother.

The big public school was always on my mind, so one day I stopped there and waited until all the kids were in class; then I went into the school office. I told the principal my father worked and could not bring me, but wanted me to enroll in the school. I went there three weeks or so before the priest came to see Dad to find out why I was not attending Catholic school. When I got home Dad beat the hell out of me and took me back to school the next day. The head brother named Eugene called me into his office and had me hold my hands one on top of the other while he came down on the top one as hard as he could with a broom handle. He got in three licks before I made my dive for the door. I made it out with him right behind me. He chased me to the main gate and then stopped. I remember I turned around from a safe distance and put my fingers, which were swollen, to my nose. I made up my mind then and there never to set foot in that school again. Next day I went to another school about ten blocks away, No. 8, and enrolled there. About a week later Dad said, "You've been playing hooky again." I said, "No, Dad. I go to No. 8 public school, and I don't care what you do, I won't go to St. John's. You can take me back, but I won't go." Dad must have seen I meant it so he said, "all right."

Joe, my older brother, kept right on going to St. John's. I guess after a few weeks, when I did not always have to have three cents or five cents for some holy card or gimcrack, Dad could see it was cheaper, so when I talked my brother Joe into going with me to No. 8 public school, Dad didn't object. After about a year at No. 8 school, I decided to go to work.

One morning instead of going to school I looked for a job. I got one, $3.50 a week as bobbin boy, ten hours a day, curling under and between machines picking up empty bobbins from the winding machines. My poor skinny knees were all sore and my head was battered from bumping it on the iron braces holding up the machines. Three days was all I could take. I quit, and it must have been my disgust at the silk mills that made me want to get away from there.

I went back to school a few days, and one day when the sun was shining brightly and it was nice and warm, I went up along the tracks of the Delaware, Lackawanna & Western railroad. I sat down on a pile of ties, watching a freight train of empty coal cars going by. It slowed down and stopped. I thought, when it starts up I'll ride it a little ways. I did—all the way to Scranton, Pennsylvania, one hundred and twenty-five miles away. The wonderful country it went through was like nothing I had ever known. I can remember now I wasn't afraid. Somehow I asked for and was given food; it seemed so easy.

I was gone that time three days before I took a train loaded with coal back home. Dad came home from work and started after me in the kitchen. I dodged and ducked him until he made me go to bed. I did, but got up in the middle of the night and slipped out. I bummed around Paterson for two or three weeks, Dad and the cops looking for me all the time. One night I was sleeping in the cellar of one of the gang when I heard Dad and the cops upstairs asking if they had seen me. I kept still until they were gone, and in the early hours of the morning I made my way over to the Erie Railroad and took the front end of a passenger train until I was put off about fifty miles out of Paterson. Boy, I was free! I walked the tracks, keeping away from the towns.

That evening I came to a hobo jungle where three or four men were cooking. I stopped and sat down. No one said a word. I wasn't scared, but I was ready to run. One fellow about forty years old was cooking some liver in an old flattened-out can. He had a little sack. He took out bread and some cheese; the coffee was already made. The other fellows were together, and they had a stew and were eating it. Christ, was I hungry, but they never said a word. The fellow with the liver took his time and when it was all ready he set it down on a clean place he had made, and he too started to eat. I was watching every bite but not saying a word. All at once he said, "Where you from, kid?" I said, "New York," and he said, "Eat yet?" I said no, and he just made a motion with his hand for me to come over and sit down, which I did. He let me clean up the biggest part of the grub.

That was how I met my first friend on the road, and in the few weeks I was with him I learned a lot. I can't remember his name now. I only remember he was clean, and I never heard him swear or use loud talk. In spite of all you hear about older men taking up with kids on the road, this hobo—and he was that, pure and simple—never made a wrong move or a dirty crack while I was with him.

After we had eaten, he asked where I was going to stay that night. I said I didn't know but guessed I would find a boxcar down the track. He said, "No, a boxcar is too hard. Wait until it's dark, and we will go over here a little ways. There's a barn full of nice soft hay." I guess he had stopped here before, because when it got dark we went about a half a mile up the tracks to a crossroad where we turned, and after a little ways we came to the barn. Inside we went up to the hayloft where we slept until early morning. When he woke me up he put his fingers to his lips for silence. We softly let ourselves down the ladder. Then he said to wait while he went over to the barn. Chickens were roosting all around, but they made no noise. When he came back we slipped out and around the barn, back to the road. I looked back and the farmer's house was only about a hundred yards away from the barn.

Down the road about a mile we stopped by a small stream where, to my surprise, he pulled six eggs out of his coat pocket. We built a fire and from his small bag he took four cans, one inside the other, a tomato can being the largest, a small milk can the smallest. We boiled the eggs and made coffee and that was breakfast. All the while he was talking about how to get by on the road, what was all right to steal, what was wrong. It seemed it was all right to steal eggs, chickens, milk, anything to eat, but never steal anything else, because it would get you in trouble. Work was something to be done only as a last resort. As long as you could eat and sleep warm without it, leave it alone.

I stayed with this tramp for almost three months. We walked all over the state of New York in the back country, and parts of Pennsylvania and Maryland. It was all a wonderland to me, and only on one occasion did we find it necessary to work in order to eat. The farmer wanted to pay me only half a man's pay, but my hobo partner said, "No, you pay him the same as me or we don't work." It was one dollar a day and bed and board. Well, it was only a small field of barley, and we had to promise to finish it or not get paid. I wanted to quit the first day, but the hobo said no, we gave our word, and we would keep it. It took about a week to cut and bundle and stack it. He handled the cradle and I bundled and shocked. The farmer paid us off, and we started out again.

I found out this hobo did not give his word lightly; when he gave it he kept it. He explained it to me by saying he felt as much like quitting that first day as I did; it was only his word he liked to keep. He found if you worked a week or two once in a while, you found out how awful it was and it would always make him renew his resolve to do as little of it as possible. He never asked me for any of my money. He did not drink, and when we bought anything like coffee, sugar, cheese or bread, we both paid our share. There never was any talk about it. He just paid the bill, then would say, "That came to a dollar, kid. You owe me fifty cents." I

11

would pay up at once. When I left this fine old hobo I still had about a dollar left, and we had been together a good many nights. We would be walking down the road when he would say, "Let's stop here a while till they go to bed at that last farm we passed. There's a fine milk house right near the barn." We would go back when everything was dark. He was never wrong; there would be a well-house or spring-house with pans of milk on the tables and benches. We never made a mess, and when we had drunk our fill, we would walk four or five miles further, just in case, and find a barn and bed down. For three months we never went near the railroads. He would say, "Too many people. The good living is in the back country."

Sometimes the farmer would get up before us and find us in the hayloft. We would always say we just met on the road the day before. A few times, because I was such a kid, the farmer would ask me to the house to eat. I never went unless my partner could go, too, and some of the feeds those back country farm wives put out were sure good: home-smoked ham or bacon and eggs, homemade bread, country butter. The farmers' wives would want to know all about me. I was always an orphan who had run away from an orphanage, and that got their sympathy every time.

Well, that was how I spent the first three months of this, my first long stay on the road. I left my friend in Bath, New York, where a farmer offered me a small sum to stay with him and help with the chores. The hobo said, "Better do it, kid; it's getting pretty close to winter, and I've got to be getting south. That's tough country down there, so better winter here." So I stayed. No goodbyes, just a wave of the hand and he was gone. I stayed with Frank—that was the farmer's name—until the grapes were picked. He had two small children, a boy five and a girl seven. They got to like me a lot. When the work was over and Frank said, "Well, kid, I guess that's all," the kids began to cry. They didn't want me to go. So Frank said, "OK! OK! I'll get him a job in town and he can board with us." So that's how I went to work for Glen H. Curtiss before he made his first flight at Bath, New York in 1908. At that time he made the Curtiss motorcycle. I swept the small plant and ran the drill press. It was Curtiss himself who showed me how to drill small pressed-paper washers for the airplane which he finally flew.

I got to wondering what it was like on the other side of the mountain, so one day with my pay in my pocket and my other shirt in a bundle, I started over the hill. I made it about twenty miles and stopped for the night with a farmer about ten miles from Horn, New York. He took me to the house and his wife put me to bed in a nice little room that used to be their son's. I thought at first I would like it there, but after about two months of doing all the work while the man sat in front of the fire in his stocking feet, I changed my mind.

They had two girls I had to drive to school every day. The oldest, about twelve or thirteen, would sit as far away from me as she could. The young one, about six or seven, was not so bad, but had to do like her sister or the older girl would tell on her. In all the time I was there I was never let into the family group. It was a house of the damnedest sourpusses I ever saw. No music, no singing, no talk, at least around me. I began to suspect that all they wanted of me was what work they could get out of me, since I was only getting board and room and, we had agreed, my clothes. I had received up till then only a pair of felt boots so I could work in the snow, chopping wood, cleaning the barn, etc., while he sat in the house. I can't recall him ever helping me with any of the chores. Well, my clothes were getting thin and worn, and I had no Sunday suit, so I told him I would have to have some new clothes. He talked to his wife and she said she would mend my old ones. That did it.

The next day, without a word, I got up and hit the road to town. No money, no overcoat, no heavy underwear, but good warm feet in my felt boots. I got into Hornell, New York. It was dark by then, so, hungry and cold with no place to go, I made for the YMCA. It was lucky I did. The man in charge gave me supper and a bed and said he would see me in the morning. The next day he told me to have breakfast, and then if I wanted to come back, he would have something for me to do. I had breakfast and for quite a while I was undecided whether to go back or not. I was done working for nothing, but then I couldn't very well hit the road with a foot of snow on it and the temperature at ten degrees below. And I thought I could always beat it if it was too much. But it turned out OK. He said I could help him around the place for my bed and meals and fifty cents a day.

Well, I stayed there about a month and never saved a thin dime. I spent my big salary as fast as I got it. Boy, did I splurge! About this time I decided to write home. After a few days I received a letter telling me my Dad was very sick, so I decided to go home. That night I took a fast Manifest Freight out of Hornell, New York. One hundred and twenty-five miles later, almost frozen, I arrived in Susquehanna, Pennsylvania. I went into the railroad shops where I got warm at one of the engines. Twenty minutes later I was between two cars, my arms around the handbrake rod and my hands in my coat pockets. I rode that Manifest into Port Jervis, New York, and then into Hoboken, New Jersey, about eight or nine hours total. I tried to get off the train when it stopped in the yards, but could hardly get my arms from around the brake rod. A railroad bull came along about then and helped me down. He took me out of the yards to a saloon where they made me a hot toddy and rubbed my hands and face with cold water. After a while I could speak. The bull asked me what the hell I was doing in that kind of weather on a fast Manifest. It was a faster train than the passenger trains on that road. When I told them I had ridden it outside all the way from Hornell, he didn't believe me at first. He said by all rights I should have been frozen stiff long ago. When I could walk, he took me to the streetcar line and gave me my fare, twenty cents, to Paterson. When I arrived home I found Dad much better.

Two
BACK COUNTRY RAMBLES

I left home shortly after finding my father was better. I left Paterson on the DL&W railroad going to Scranton, Pennsylvania. There I found a county fair going on. I hung around this fair as it moved from town to town and somehow managed to eat by selling peanuts and popcorn from a basket all over the fairgrounds. I slept in the stables at the racetrack found at every fair grounds. I don't know how many little towns in Pennsylvania and Maryland we made before we moved on to Hagerstown, Maryland. I knew this was to be the last fair in that part of the country and the next one would be at Columbus, South Carolina.

It was at Hagerstown around 1904 or 1905 that I had my first lesson in discrimination and was first made alert to the deep hatred some people had for Negroes and, in fact, for anyone who in any way had anything to do with them. At some little town along the way I had made the acquaintance of a young Negro boy about my own age; I am sure I was not more than eleven or twelve at the time. As I remember, he did a little work around the stables. He told me horses were wonderful, and he loved being around them. He had no steady stable to work for, but made enough to eat on odd jobs when he could find them.

I stumbled on him one night in the dark. I was looking for a place to sleep. As I entered the empty stall, I heard a noise and standing very still I held my breath, trying to make out just what it was. I was not exactly afraid, but was ready to run at the first sign of danger. I guess he must have been holding his breath the same as I was. At any rate, he moved first and said, "What do you want?"

I let out my breath in one deep sigh, for I could tell this was not a man, but a boy more frightened than I was. I said I didn't know there was anyone there; I was just looking for a place to sleep. He told me this was the only stall not in use, but I could stay there if I wanted. I wanted to, and thus began a friendship which grew out of our common needs and the misery of cold nights when the warmth of our bodies lying close on a pile of straw was the only blanket we had. I had never had contact with a Negro before, and because there must have been very few at that time in my part of my home town, I was not innoculated with the prejudices that grownups usually instill in children. I felt none of it. I liked my friend and didn't even consider his color, and when I began to feel a coldness on the part of the people connected with the fair who had been quite friendly before, I did not for some time understand what it was all about.

It was my little friend who wised me up. One night at Hagerstown I was telling him about the fellow I worked for, selling peanuts and candy, etc., and how he hardly spoke to me any more, and I didn't know what was the matter. This boy looked at me and said, "Don't you-all know?" I said I hadn't done anything. He said, "You-all been seen playing around with me." Next day I had proof of how right he was.

About ten o'clock, before the crowds were large enough to sell anything around the grounds, I went to the stand of my boss and stood around waiting for my basket of peanuts, popcorn and candy. He said nothing for a long time, and I kept standing there, waiting. All at once he shouted, "What the hell you want, you goddamn nigger-lover?" I stood with my mouth open. What could I say? What could I do? There were other fair people within hearing. They watched me as the tears ran down my dirty face.

There was another person at the stand, a lady, who the fair people said was laying my boss. She had never said much to me in the months I had peddled peanuts for him. But every once in a while she would slip me a few dimes out of the

16

change box behind the peanut-stand. She looked at my boss and said, "For Christ's sake, he's only a kid! Why the hell don't you let him alone?"

He said, "He's a goddamn nigger-lover; he's been sleeping with that nigger down in the barns."

"So what?" she said, "he's made plenty of nickels for you. He's a good salesman, so what the hell do you care?" She said she would fix up my basket for me. They were still fighting when I told her thanks and turned around and walked off.

I went back to the stables and helped my friend carry water to the horses. When the fair ended in Hagerstown, he went to some ranch where he had landed a job as an exercise boy. I never saw him again. I left with the intention of catching up with the fair in Columbus, South Carolina.

I took the Seaboard Airline Railroad through Virginia, North Carolina, and points south, and tougher country I have never encountered before or since. I knew nothing at that time of southern chain gangs. On this trip I saw them at work. I can still see the chains and the looks of beaten misery on the faces of the prisoners. It was only my age that stopped them from putting me on one, but even they dared not chain up a twelve-year-old boy, and a white boy at that! But I don't think they would have had a moment's hesitation had I been a Negro.

I got through Virginia without mishap, but at Raleigh, North Carolina, I was caught in the freight yards by a railroad cop, taken to jail and held three days. No trial, no nothing, just held in jail. On the third day, another cop took me back to the same railroad and told me to get the next freight east. I told him I didn't want to go east. He said to get the hell out of the South. "There's enough damn Yankee bums down here already!"

Well, I took the next freight headed east. But about a mile down the track, I jumped off and, going around the town, hopped the next freight going south. I made it to Columbus, South Carolina, but the fair was over, and I could not learn where it had gone from there. I was two days in Columbus; I almost starved to death. Talk about your southern hospitality. Hell, they slammed the door in my face as soon as they heard my New Jersey accent.

So I went to the colored part of town, and I was never turned down for something to eat. Sometimes it wasn't much, but it was a part of what they had, and there were a few times when I know they cooked something special for me.

Well, I had my fill of the South. I headed back east, the same way I had come. I rode the Seaboard Airline. On the front end of the fastest passenger train out of Columbus, I made it all the way to Seaboard, North Carolina, where a cop pulled me off early in the morning. Seaboard was such a small town that I wondered what he was going to do with me. He wasn't a bad cop, but a typical country one. I think he thought I was a runaway from some rich family back east. I sat around the depot with him until about eight a.m. when the agent came to work. He asked where I was from and telegraphed to Paterson, New Jersey, asking if I was wanted there. About two hours later he had an answer: "McGuckin not wanted here." It seems he had not given my age, or any other details, so there was no other answer he could get. I suppose the Paterson police simply looked up the criminals wanted list, and I wasn't on it.

Then out of a clear blue sky he said, "Well, how in hell are you going to pay me for that telegram?" I said I didn't send any telegram.

"Don't make any difference," he said. "It was about you, and I'm going to find you something to do so you can pay me back."

There was a small hotel just across from the depot. He took me there and they needed a bellhop and all-around boy, so I was it. I'll never forget that little hotel, only about six rooms and family style cooking. The two colored ladies in the kitchen almost killed me with food. And such food!— home cooked ham, bacon, and home-smoked sausage, pound cakes, eggs, thick steaks and chicken. My God, how they could cook it! Every time I passed that kitchen one or the other of them was stuffing me with food. Of course, I was tall and skinny, and the oldest lady would say, "You're so poorly, boy. We-all's got to fatten you up." The other one never said much. The only thing I can remember her saying was, "You all hungry, boy?" with her hands full of something for me to eat even though she knew it was just a little while since the other one had stuffed me with smoked sausage, fried ham, eggs, and hot biscuits until it was running out of my ears. I could have grown to love those two old colored ladies.

Well, about a week later the owner of the hotel, a very slow maneuvering sort of elderly gentleman with a small Vandyke silver moustache and beard, called me into the office, which was also the lobby, front room, etc., and said he would have to let me go. He said I was too fast. Every time he called me I moved so fast he just couldn't stand it. Nobody was ever made to move that fast. Must be something wrong with me, and anyway, he didn't know why he let that constable talk him into needing a bellboy. If there was one thing his hotel didn't need, it was a bellboy, especially one who was eating him out of all the profits, which I admit must have been true.

But he wasn't a bad old goat. He gave me three dollars and told me to get something to eat in the kitchen and find some other place to stay. I went to the kitchen and they stuffed me again, and when I was ready to leave, the oldest lady gave me a lunch to take with me. I looked at it and was half scared out of my wits. My God, it looked like she had wrapped up the kitchen stove and thrown in the icebox and a few more odds and ends. The package must have been two feet square. The other one was stuffing my pockets with apples, dried peaches and raisins. She said it was good food for a growing boy. By this time the two of them were blowing their noses and tears were running down their faces. In one short week I had become their honey child.

I took the lunch and, looking like I was carrying away half of the hotel in my arms and pockets, with a lump in my throat and the tears streaming down my face, I went out the back way, made the railroad track and, walking as fast as I could, I left Seaboard behind me.

After about three or four miles, I came to a siding where cordwood was stacked up in piles along the tracks. Here I met three colored children, a boy about ten and two girls about eight and nine. I stopped, and after talking with them a while, I decided to see what was in my lunch. Christ, there was enough to last all the way to Richmond, Virginia, where I had decided to go, but I knew I couldn't carry it and still catch a freight if I had to run for it. I asked the kids if they were hungry. They were shy, and also I was a white boy, so I sat down on a bunch of cordwood and said, "I've got too much here, you-all better help me eat it."

First one, then the others came closer and looked at that big lunch. The boy said, "Where you-all get all that stuff?" I told them, and slowly he came over and sat down, followed by the girls. We cleared up that lunch and the raisins, dried peaches and apples as well.

Soon we were playing tag around those cordwood piles. They were too fast for me. They got me "it" right away, and they laughed at me when I tried to catch and tag one of them. I quit after a while and told them I had to get going or I'd be caught out in the woods that night.

They held a small council of some sort; then the boy said, "You-all can stay with us tonight. You all can sleep in where we sleeps." So, with mixed feelings of I knew not what, I went with them.

Not far from the cordwood piles, a road crossed the tracks, just a dirt rut road. They turned off and about a mile down this road, we came to their place, a shanty, about two rooms and a shed in back. The old grampa was sick and all crippled up, but he made me welcome, and that night I slept on a blanket in front of the fireplace. I had to get up quite a few times to put wood on the fire because the old man couldn't. Although he never asked me to do it, each time he would thank me kindly. I did it, I guess, because the shanty would have been too cold if I hadn't, and I wanted to be warm, too.

Next morning the kids called me at about six o'clock and I went into the shed, a lean-to, which was where they cooked and ate. Their big sister, about eighteen or nineteen, made me welcome. She was making breakfast—hominy grits and fat side pork, and cornbread. I sure loved their cornbread and blackstrap molasses.

After breakfast we played around until about noon. I went with the boy while he looked at his rabbit-traps, boxes with a trigger arrangement. He caught two rabbits that morning which we took home and skinned and cleaned. Then we walked down to the railroad tracks and back to the cordwood piles. There we found an old man with an oxcart and ox, loading cordwood. It was light cordwood so we could handle it OK. When we had finished he asked me if I would like to come home with him and work on his plantation. Just help with the chores, he said. Said he had a boy, Charlie, about my age.

I went home with him and after about three or four days found that "helping with the chores" consisted of slopping the pigs, feeding the mules and ox, cleaning out the barns, chopping wood and filling the kitchen woodboxes, and carrying water from the well. After this little bit of exercise, which began about five-thirty a.m., we had breakfast, and then proceeded to split rails and cut cordwood for ten hours, with a break of fifteen minutes to eat the lunch we carried. After supper, I would help Charlie with his homework. All this for board and room and clothes. But I liked Charlie and stayed at this place about three months.

Until one night at supper old man Yates, who fought the Civil War in my presence every time he got the chance, was bragging about the battles that the South won, how they routed the damn Yankees. I just didn't think when I said to him, "Mr. Yates, how is it you licked the Yankees so bad and lost the war?'' I didn't know it was coming or I would have been ready for it, but the old devil caught me unaware and smacked me hard across the face.

No one said a word. I looked at him and he at me. I pushed back my chair and left the house. No hat, no coat, just as I was. Charlie came out after me and cried when I told him I was leaving. I left right then and there and only went as far as the next farm where I found a shed still half-full of cotton where I slept until morning.

I knew the kids on this small and poor farm. In the morning when I heard them I came out of the shed and up to the house. There were three kids, two little girls and a boy. They crowded around me and wanted to know all about what happened. The man and wife were more impatient to hear than the kids. I told them and the kids began to shout , ''Can't he stay here, Paw? Aw, stay with us, Henry!'' Well, the man said OK. He didn't like old man Yates anyway, and the woman was pleased. Thus another three months or more was spent with these good people.

They didn't have as much to feed me as Yates, but I was given the same as their own kids and slept with their boy, and I was not worked to death. In fact, they wanted me to go to school with the boy, but I wouldn't go. I said I could help better by staying home—which was a damn lie, because after a week or two I found a good place to fish, and used to sneak off and be gone all day. But I always brought back a lot of fish, and they loved them. Never said a word about me running off. In fact, the old man wanted to go with me sometime, but he never did.

One day I just took off and hiked about twenty miles or so until I came to a large plantation. As I was hungry by this time, I went up to the big house—about fifteen rooms. It must have been one of the old mansions of the days before the Civil War. In fact, they were later to brag that it had once worked over one hundred slaves. The lady at the house called to someone inside that there was a boy outside who wanted something to eat. Christ! Out they came. I don't remember just how many after this long a time, but I think there were seven or eight boys. They were all the way from about eight or nine to twenty-three or twenty-four years old. The oldest ones had their wives with them. They crowded around me just looking. Outside of the wives there were no girls. I didn't know what I had gotten into, but after looking me over for what seemed like a heck of a long time, one of the older men said, "Well, come on in; we were just eating supper." So they all filed back inside. I went with them into a big long room, both kitchen and dining-room together, with a Negro woman at the stove and another serving the table. All the man said was, "Sit!" But where? Every chair was filled. Then he said, "Get yourself a chair and sit." So I got myself a chair and sat.

Then came the questions; they asked me everything they could think of about myself. Their father had died, I found out later, and the plantation had been divided among the children, the oldest one running it and dividing the profits. It sure was a big place as I remember, over one thousand acres.

Well, that night they must have held a pow-wow, and the next morning I found I was the sole property of the oldest brother and was to help him with his part of the farm work. I don't know how they decided this as I didn't ask to stay, but the kids were fun, and after a few days I kind of liked it. They sure ate good, and they did get me some new work-clothes. I enjoyed myself there for most of the winter, and it gets cold there—make no mistake about that. I helped with the stock, getting wood, fence-building, etc., but they didn't work such long hours in the winter, and as there were so many to help, everything was done by about four o'clock. Then all of us would be out by the big barn waiting for supper if it wasn't too cold.

I remember one day they were riding some of the mules, and, believe me, those young mules could run. Well, they were all bragging about how well they could ride. They asked me, "Can you ride?" Can I ride? Didn't I ride in almost every race from Scranton, Pennsylvania, to Columbus, South Carolina? Well, I guess I laid it on too thick. Anyway, right in the middle of my telling about the last race I won on a very mean horse one of them came up leading a young mule all saddled and ready to go.

What could I do? Hell, I never had anything more to do with a horse than to feed him his oats at the front end and take them away later from the rear. But I thought, hell, anybody can ride. So I walked over to this mule and tried to get on. But he wouldn't let me get my foot up. As soon as I put any weight against him, he would move away. One of the kids yelled, ''Hey, maybe they get on a racehorse that way, but down here we get on from the other side!'' I had never known there was any difference. I tried the other side and the mule stood still while I got aboard.

The most I could get out of that critter was something between a walk and a slow dog-trot. We ambled to the gate about three hundred yards away, and they were all yelling, ''Look at him go!'' I turned him around, and then it happened. My heels must have caught him just right, for all at once that mule was a streak of lightning. I was out of the saddle, on the horn, around his neck, and when he got within a few feet of the yelling kids—and all the women who were outside by now taking it all in—he put on the brakes and I went over that mule's head as graceful as a bird and landed right at the feet of the kids. Boy, did they razz me! I said, ''How did you expect me to hold on with a saddle like that? I'm used to a racing saddle,'' and then the bell rang for supper and I was saved because they had no time for talk or kidding when they were eating. They just ate.

It was just a few weeks after this that they began to talk of plowing. It seems they planted a few hundred acres of peanuts. The land was sandy and light, so my first day of plowing went fairly well. But the field kept getting bigger and bigger to me instead of smaller and smaller. I began to look for ways to get out of plowing, and one day I just unhitched the mule and led him home. The brother I was working for met me at the barn. I told him that Jenny was sick or something, wouldn't pull the plow. Hell, in that soil, now that I think back, even a sick mule could have run away with the plow.

The brother said, "That's funny. She don't look sick. Let's take her out and I'll try."

Well, he took her out and that was that. He knew, but he said maybe she just wanted to rest a while. I said, "Yeah. I guess so."

I plowed all that week, but one morning instead of plowing I just wandered off and went fishing. There was a swamp about a mile or so from the barn and I had never seen so many fish. Bass, pickerel, and perch. I only had worms and a small hook, so I caught perch. I could hardly carry them back. No one said anything when I wandered in at about six o'clock, but next morning I was back to plowing again. I couldn't stand it any longer. First a half mile one way, then a half mile back, and each time only about eight inches plowed. That afternoon about two o'clock I unhitched the mule and tied him to the fence by the gate where I knew they would find him, and I took off across country for the railroad. I was going back home for a while.

I caught a freight that night and landed in Richmond, Virginia, next morning. I found a place to wash up a little and went sight-seeing around town. Towards evening I was getting pretty hungry so I decided to try my luck panhandling. I waited on a corner, watching people go by and trying to get up enough courage to ask one of them for the price of something to eat. I had never begged anyone like that before. I had always gone to houses and asked for some work to earn something to eat, but this time I decided to try my luck this way.

I would pick out a man walking toward me and decide, "I'll ask this one." But when he got close I always let him pass with some excuse to myself that he didn't look right,

25

or he might be a cop, or one thing and another. Truth was, I lost my nerve each time. I decided on about thirty or forty different men, never a woman, and discarded them all as bad risks. Then I noticed a large man just standing there as I was, and it came to me he had been standing there almost as long as I had. He didn't seem to be watching me, but I had a funny feeling about him. It was getting late, however, and I had to eat, so cop or no cop, I thought, "Here goes." I went over to him and started to ask him, but about as far as I got was, "Mister, would you. . ." Then I was stuck.

He was looking at me with a funny kind of look, not mean or stern, just a kind of a look that said, "Well?" Just as I was about to turn away he said, "What's the matter, kid? Lost your nerve?"

"No," I said, "but I never bummed anyone on the street before. I'm sure hungry."

He smiled. "That's just what I thought. I've been watching you, and I wondered just how long it was going to take you to get up enough nerve to brace somebody. Where you from?"

I told him.

"And where you going?"

I told him I had been away for almost two years, and I thought I'd go home for a while.

He said, "Good idea. Let's you and I take a little walk."

So we walked. I thought: I hope they haven't fed them yet at the jail. I thought sure that's where we were headed. But when we passed first one cop and then another, I began to try and figure out what I'd gotten myself into. The next block I found out. We came to a large drugstore, and he said, "Let's go in here for a while."

We did. The druggist, a nice elderly man greeted him with, "Hello there, I see you got one."

"Yeah," he said, "found him down on the corner trying to get up enough nerve to bum someone for the price of supper."

Then he turned to me and said, "Charlie will take care of you. Don't be afraid," and he left me there with the druggist. This fellow got a book and started to question me: name, address, parents living? How long away from home? Why I ran away, etc., etc.

Well, when he was through he said, "So you think you want to go home for a while, do you?" When I said yes, he said, "That's good. It will save some trouble as long as you want to go." He ran some sort of organization which kept a lookout for runaway boys and girls, and I walked right into it.

A little later he locked the store and we went to a nearby restaurant. He said, "Sit down and order what you want. Don't be afraid to order enough to eat, but eat it." Well, I did. When I was through, he took me across the street to a small hotel. He said, "We are going to trust you since you were going home anyhow. You will have a room here tonight, and in the morning go back to the restaurant and they will give you breakfast. At nine o'clock you come to the drugstore and we will see what we can do to help you get home."

When I arrived at the store next morning, he was already there and so was the man I met on the street. They greeted me just like one fellow greets another. "Have a good night's sleep? Did you enjoy your breakfast?" After a while, the first man I met asked if I ever sailed on a big ship. I said I'd never been in any thing bigger than a rowboat. "Well," he said, "come along. We're going down and see a real ship."

It was a big ship, and we went aboard. He took me to the kitchen, "the galley," as I was later to learn, where the steward met us. He said, "Here he is." That was all. He put out his hand and said, "This man here will take care of you," and was gone. The steward put me to work peeling potatoes. I didn't know where the ship was going, but I had pictures of China and the South Seas in my mind.

Not long after I boarded, the ship backed out of the pier and started for open water. I was on my way. I peeled potatoes. I peeled onions. I peeled carrots. I just peeled and peeled until I began to feel a sort of funny feeling in my stomach. It got worse and worse, and before long I was really sick. They put me in a bunk in one of the cabins and left me there. After a while I went to sleep.

When I woke up the boat was still. We were stopped. I got up and went on deck and found we were tied up at a big wharf. I asked a sailor where we were and he said, "New York, son. This ship has only two places to go. One is New York; the other is Richmond, Virginia." Boy, did I feel cheated: It was an outrage! How could they do that to me! Here I am all set for China, ports east and ports west, and they land me twenty miles from home! The steward handed me money enough to take the ferry to New Jersey and the streetcar home, and that was that.

It is a strange thing as I write this to find that Paterson leaves me with so few memories to write about. Paterson always seemed to me to be a city where people just worked from one day to the next and had no life of their own that was not at the beck and call of the hundreds of mill-whistles that blew to tell you when to wake up, when to report to work, when to eat lunch, and when to go home. I think this was one reason I hated that town.

Even the little things I can remember did not happen so much in Paterson itself as in the outskirts, like Lakeview. Where the lake was in Lakeview I don't know to this day, and I doubt there was a lake there, or if there was, I couldn't find it. Then there was the country outside the city. This part I must admit I liked. There were small streams I found for myself three or four miles up the railroad track of the Erie Railroad. Little streams no wider than a small ditch, but filled with the best watercress I have ever seen. I used to take a large basket out there and make bunches of watercress and sell them back in town for a nickel a bunch. I made a dollar now and again this way.

I was also the ice-cream king of Jackson Street. A stolen can of thick condensed milk, a spoonful of vanilla, some sugar, water, rock salt, and some ice I swiped off the ice-wagons and I was in business. I never did have any left over. Maybe my experience in the ice cream business is responsible for my not liking ice cream very much today. I never ate any of my own, either.

Sometime after my return from the South I had my first and last experience as a paid actor. I was just wandering around the outskirts of Paterson and suddenly saw this big sign way up in the air, "Fairyland." Boy, was I in heaven that only those who have traveled with a fair or carnival can know. It was early, and there was no one watching the gate, so I just walked in and started to look around. After taking in the whole place, I was sitting on the steps of a large building with a sign, "Theatre." A fellow came along and said, "Hello, kid. What you doing?"

I said, "Nothing."

He said, "Don't you go to school?"

"No, I just got back home from down south."

He said, "We have our act here for a week. If you don't go to school, I can give you a job." I asked, doing what? He was a wise one. He said, "Acting." He said they had to have a young boy about my age in the act, so if I wanted to, I could get fifty cents each performance and a dollar on Wednesday, Saturday and Sunday when there were two shows, afternoon and night. I was frightened, but I don't think I would have passed it up even if he had said, "Of course, we have to horsewhip you every show."

Well, I hung around there all afternoon. The cop on duty asked me what I was doing there. I said, "I'm with the show in here. I'm an actor." He looked at me kind of funny and said OK.

Well, about seven o'clock I went to the back door of the theater. The man at the door must have been told I'd be around, because when I told him I was going to act in the show he laughed and said, "Sure, kid. They're in there waiting for you. Better hurry; they can't start the show till you git there." Getting there meant going down some dark stairs to a dressing room. One of them was all made up like what everyone thinks looks like a tramp. But I'd seen too many real tramps, and this fellow just looked to me like a real funny circus clown. The other fellow was dressed like a train conductor. I went in, and they asked me if I was afraid. No, I wasn't afraid. Oh, no, not much! I felt like running as fast as I could to get out of there. I don't know, but I suspect they knew I felt that way. One or the other one stayed right close to me telling me not to worry. After the first time, I'd see how easy it was and it took kids like me to make real actors. Why, wasn't that the way *they* began?

"Sure was," said the tramp.

"Sure was," said the conductor.

They kept telling me what I had to do. "Just do what we tell you. Don't speak, yours is a silent part. Look sad." And they made me look sad, and then nearly busted their sides laughing. "That's good! Boy, oh boy, he's the best kid we ever found. We'll have to keep him with us."

Little by little my fright was leaving me. We went upstairs. They showed me the drop-curtain with painted boxcars and door. Behind the door were a couple of planks on wooden horses which was the floor of the boxcar. After what seemed like a long time their turn came. The tramp was holding on to me in back of the drop, waiting for the cue, but later I knew he was taking no chances on my bolting. The conductor walked slowly on the stage, supposedly taking down the numbers of the cars on the train. While he was doing this to soft music, the tramp, at a certain part of the music, dropped a brick on the floor. This made the conductor look in the car door, and he shouted, "Come out of there you bum!" I walked the planks and climbed down through the boxcar door to the stage. The conductor held on to me like the tramp did. I know they were afraid I'd run, because after I showed up for the next show the following night, they did not lay their hands on me.

Well, while I had no part to speak but just stood there, I can remember almost all of that little act. Not too funny,

I suppose, but not too bad, either. They were good dancers, and the tramp was a good singer. After pulling me out of the boxcar door, the conductor bawled me out for riding his freight, when he saw a piece of paper sticking out of my coat pocket. "What is this?" he said. "Oh, a telegram." He read it out loud. When he got through, he was saying how sorry he was that my mother was dying, and just then the audience began to laugh. I couldn't figure it, because the guy almost had me crying. I looked around and there in the boxcar door was just a head looking first one way, then the other. The conductor shouted for the tramp to come out of there, so he came out. It was a high door, just about as high as a real boxcar, but the tramp just stepped down like it was a few inches. I don't know how he did that so gracefully and yet so funny. Well, they went on with arguments, jokes and songs, and I got to enjoy my part, even though I never did anything except look sad. I got pretty good at that.

After Sunday night's show they gave me an extra fifty cents and told me they were going back home until they got another booking and they might look me up sometime. They never did, of course, and that was the beginning and end of my career as an actor.

A group of Wobblies in the 1910s, probably out West. In the top row, extreme left, is Henry McGuckin; at the far right is William D. "Big Bill" Haywood.

Three
WOBBLY

Not long after this, Paterson began to pall on me again. Dad was working at Susquehanna, Pennsylvania. I left Paterson on the Erie Railroad and made Susquehanna the next day, and had no trouble getting a job in the boiler shop where my Dad was a handyman, which in those days meant he was a damn good boilermaker. But they could pay him less by calling him a handyman. It wasn't long before I had my bellyfull of that boiler shop and I told my Dad, "I'm going to quit, Dad; this is not for me."

He said, "Where you off to now?"

I told him, "This time I think I will go to the Pacific Coast. I've heard a lot about it."

Well, he gave me twenty dollars and told me to buy a ticket as far as that would go. I did it. Paid for a ticket to Minneapolis. There I took a few days to look around. I had a few dollars left and they didn't last long.

I landed a job at Midway, a freight dispatch terminal half way between Minneapolis and St Paul. I was too young and not strong enough for the rugged work, but I stuck it out for as long as the boss would let me. On payday he told me he was sorry but he couldn't keep me any longer. Well, board and room had taken about all I made, and it wasn't long before I was broke again.

There was a small office of the YMCA at Midway, and one day I just strolled in there and asked the secretary for a job. He looked me over and said, "Run away from home?"

"No," I said, "my folks know where I am. I'm on my way out west."

"Well," he told me, "I'm going to do a lot of landscaping around this place, and if you want, you can help me. Pay a dollar a day and board and room.''

Hell, that was more than I made at the freight dispatch. There you got two dollars for ten hours, and board and room was a dollar twenty-five a day at the boarding house. So I took the job. I stayed about four months until we finished the landscaping and he couldn't find anything more for me to do.

One day he asked me if I knew anybody in Washington. I told him my brother ran a hotel in Wilbur, Washington. ''Why don't you wire to see if he's got a job for you?'' So I did. A few days later I received a ticket by wire and fifty dollars to come to Wilbur. So I packed up my bag with my extra shirt and pair of socks, and within four days I was on the soil of the State of Washington.

My brother put me to work as dishwasher and all-around flunky. It was here that I began to break into the cooking racket. My brother was a ball-player, and he was hired from time to time to pitch for a team in some other part of the state. He would just go and tell me to take over. ''Just make everything taste good and it will be OK.'' And by golly, it was! But I was quick to find out that working for a member of your family was not the easiest thing to do, and after several beefs about one thing or another, I walked out of town one day and didn't go back.

I went to Medical Lake, Washington, where I hired out as an attendant at the Eastern Washington Hospital for the Insane. I was there almost a year, taking care of the lawn and flowers. One fellow I had on the gang would run as fast as he could to the lawn every morning. There he would be on his knees picking up things and putting them into his mouth. I asked what he was doing.

''I'm getting worms,'' he said. ''Why not? The birds eat them. I have to hurry and get mine or the damn birds will get them all.''

After I worked there for a few months, I was chosen to sing at the Wednesday night ''movies'' with the colored slides they used in those days—songs such as ''Won't You Come

Over to My House and Play," "You're My Little Girl," "Roses Bring Memories of Your Beautiful Garden of Roses." I finally quit and headed for Seattle and the wide Pacific.

I made my way slowly across the state, stopping to work in the hayfields here and there until I finally landed in Seattle. For some time I did fairly well. I was able, after many trips to the waterfront and standing in the gangs of longshoremen, to be picked out quite a few times to work a ship, mostly unloading cases of salmon from Alaska, and then loading the ship again with sacks of sugar or cement. It was hard work, but the pay was better than I had ever received. You worked a ship until it was unloaded and loaded again, sometimes forty-eight to fifty hours with only time enough out to eat meals. You were paid at the end of each ship-loading. So I made enough to live and have a room in a waterfront hotel.

One night in January, 1912, while not working, I wandered down to the slave market, as it was called, where there were employment offices crowded close together for two or three blocks, interspersed with saloons, hock-shops, and clothing stores for workers. Seeing a crowd on a corner, I stopped to listen to a soapboxer who was speaking about industrial unionism and the free-speech fight then going on in Aberdeen, Washington (1911-1912). After he was through, he invited all those who wished to know more about unionism to come to the IWW hall where there would be another speaker. I was very interested. I followed this soapboxer to the hall where a fellow worker named Floyd spoke, followed by Tommy Whitehead. I was sold before the meeting was half over. Floyd was a wonderful speaker who could make you understand because of the way he had of explaining the complicated theories of industrial unionism in simple language, and by his comparisons with craft unionism.

At the end of his talk, he called for volunteers to go to Aberdeen to help fill the jails and win back free speech and the right to organize. I was not a member so I asked Tommy Whitehead if I could go and help. After some time, while he talked with Floyd and some others, he said, "What's your name, son?"

I told him.

He said, "You know you might not only be thrown into jail? You could be beaten up."

I said, "I'll take my chances with the rest of them."

He called a few fellows over and told them, "The kid wants to go along." None of them objected.

About midnight some eleven or twelve of us left the hall. We went to a cheap restaurant where one of the men paid for "coffee and" for all of us. Then we got a streetcar and went to the freight yard where we boarded a freight headed for Aberdeen. The next day, when we were within ten miles of Aberdeen, we all jumped off and went one at a time by different routes into Aberdeen. We would leave after a talk with the fellow in charge. I found out, when my turn came, that what had been troubling me all the time—how we were to contact the other free-speech fighters in Aberdeen—had been taken care of, but no one was told until the last moment, and each one of us was to make contact at a different place. This way if one of us was a stool-pigeon, he could not tell the cops where the other fellows were to be met. I was to go to a certain street-corner and stand around there for at least ten minutes. I had a common straight-pin in the lapel of my coat with neither the head nor the point showing; just the little part of the pin could be seen in the opening of the buttonhole of the lapel.

I went across country a mile or so until I came to a well-traveled road and hiked my way into town. After considerable wandering around I found the corner. We were not to ask anyone for directions as this would be a dead giveaway and we would be pinched at once. The other part of my being identified was that after I had stood on the corner for the required time I was to walk down the block where I would find a pool-hall. I was to go inside and find a seat near the second table from the door. I did all this, I found the pool-hall, went in, and there were seats along the wall. I picked one out in what I thought was the right spot. There were three or four others sitting around, but no one near me. I had not been there long when another young fellow came in, sat down next to me and began to talk about the weather, finding a job, and everything but what I was waiting to hear. When I was getting afraid I had missed my contact, he said, "Here's a dime. Take the streetcar on the next corner to Hoquiam [a small town adjoining Aberdeen] and go to this address and they will tell you what's up." Then he gave me the password.

I had made contact. I took the dime and followed his directions and, arriving at the house, I knocked on the door. A fellow came and opened it. It was quiet as hell, and I thought he was the only one there. He said, "What do you want?"

I said, "Do you want to buy some corn?"

At that he smiled and said, "It's OK, fellows." And I was escorted inside where instead of this one fellow, there was hardly room to move around. There were at least thirty or forty in the house.

I had supper that night at the house, a two-story affair which shortly before had been one of the biggest whore-houses in those parts. Supper consisted of bread, brown beans, and coffee and was, as I remember, very limited.

As I had just arrived and had had no sleep the night before, I was not picked to go back to Aberdeen that night. About twenty of the boys left about seven o'clock. About ten p.m. two of them came back. They had been beaten up. One of them had been hit on the head with a pick-handle and was hurt pretty bad. The others were all in the can.

The next day passed slowly—coffee and stale donuts for breakfast and not enough beans and bread for supper. About two p.m., after ten or twelve more fellows had arrived, I was told to go upstairs to one of the rooms where fifteen of us were given instructions for that night.

We left at about seven p.m. and stationed ourselves at different parts of the main street in Aberdeen. At eight o'clock the first meeting started. There were about four or five of us in each spot, as this made the cops and the vigilantes' pick-handle brigade run from one part of town to another. We were concentrated in about four blocks, some on one side of the street, some on the other. When the first speaker began, it was about ten minutes before the cops and vigilantes arrived and began to swing their clubs and pick handles. I didn't know it at the time, but that night marked the beginning of the end of the free-speech fight.

We waited on our corner for them to arrest the bunch a block up the street, but they would merely pull them off the box and club them. After a while we saw what was happening, and, to take the heat from the boys up the street, we started our meeting. We began by singing "Solidarity Forever," and the crowd started in our direction. Singing could also be heard from halfway up the next block. They had started, too. Some of the pickhandle boys and cops came our way, some went the other. While they were laying about them, hitting not only us Wobblies but people in the crowd as well, still another meeting began further up the street. We had them running back and forth, first one place, then the other.

I was second on the box at my corner and, after my opening words, "Fellow workers," I was pushed off the box by a big vigilante. I ducked into the crowd and mixed with it, and received only one clout across the shoulder from a cop's club. When our meeting was pretty well busted up, we hollered, "There's another meeting!" and started running for the next corner. Some of the crowd would always follow, and we'd start again. After about thirty minutes of this the crowds began to thin out, and even the pickhandle brigade melted away. We made our way back to the house at Hoquiam, and those who were cut or bruised were taken care of.

The next day the city fathers asked for a committee to talk things over. After five or six days of meetings, the fight was called off—and the Wobblies had won another round.

I was not feeling well these last few days and one day while I was walking down the street I got very dizzy. I saw a doctor's office and went in. I had a hard time making it upstairs to the waiting room. A nurse asked me what was wrong. I started to tell her, but must have passed out because I came to in the hospital about half an hour later. The doctor never told me what was wrong, but he did say I was undernourished and needed a few days rest. He left orders that I was to have plenty of milk and all I wanted to eat, and for five days I was a guest at this hospital. On the fifth day the doctor said, "I think you will be OK now, son. Just take care of yourself, drink plenty of milk and you will be fine." I told him I had no money and no way to pay him. He said, "This is on me, son. Forget it." So I left and headed back to Seattle.

I headed straight for the IWW hall. I sat around a while, reading, when Tommy Whitehead called me over to his desk and told me there was a bunch leaving for Vancouver, British Columbia, where there was another free-speech fight going on. I told him to count me in. He handed me a red card and said the business meeting the night before had voted to give a card and one month's dues to any non-member who had taken part in the Aberdeen fight. So I became a member of the Industrial Workers of the World.

Six or seven of us left that night. We rode the freights to Sedro Woolley where we went into the jungles, washed up, cooked a mulligan, and made plans to get across the border into Canada. The next day we left a freight about six or eight miles from Sumas on the Canadian border. It was a long hike around Sumas and we went in pairs. Some time that night my fellow worker and I crossed into Canada and cut back to the railroad. We walked most of the night and at daylight had not yet reached the railroad. We hid out in an old deserted shack in a field until dark and started out again. We hit the railroad about thirty miles inside the border and we were safe. We landed in Vancouver the next day.

The only way we had of making contact was to go to the park where the meetings were to be held and wait until one started. There were a few free-lancers holding a meeting there as well as one Socialist meeting which the police did not interfere with. I was listening to the Socialist speaker who would make a statement and then ask the crowd for the answer. I noticed one fellow, a large man, very English, who always had the answer, and it always was the right one. At least the Socialist speaker never got to answer his own questions. So after several of these exchanges the speaker said, "The comrade seems to have all the answers, I wonder if he would like to get up here and take over." So the fellow got up on the soapbox and from that day to this I have never heard a better or clearer presentation of industrial unionism and socialism than this man gave. I learned later he was both a member of the Socialist Party of Canada and the Vancouver branch of the IWW. His name was Jack Graves.

Jack was responsible for my first real insight and understanding of the class struggle and the structure of industrial and craft unionism. Many nights in the future I was to sit by the jungle fire and listen for hours while he talked, and with a stick in the dirt, by the light of the fire, he would trace out the evolution from craft to industrial unionism. Those were lessons I never forgot, obtained in the jungle classroom. Big Professor Jack Graves, Oxford and Princeton. He carried his sheepskins in a pouch around his waist and to listen to him was to know, at once, they were not phony.

But back to the park. While I was listening to Graves, I saw a small crowd suddenly gather a little way further down the park, and in a few minutes I heard a burst of song as they opened the meeting:

> *We meet today in freedom's cause,*
> *And raise our standard high.*
> *We'll all join hands in Union strong*
> *to battle or to die.*
>
> *Hold the fort, for we are coming,*
> *Union men be strong.*
> *Side by side we battle onward,*
> *Victory will come!*

I started for the meeting. I had just arrived at the edge of the crowd when it began. The Mounted Police came from all sides with long nightsticks they used on everybody. You had to watch so that their horses wouldn't trample you. I made a dive for a bunch of bushes where I thought I'd be safe, but I had to get out of there because those damn horses went through the bushes like they weren't there. No one else could get started to speak. Someone yelled to scatter, and we did. In all directions.

That night I found the Wobbly hall and slept there. No one, it seemed, was badly hurt, but the next day we learned that some had received serious head wounds.

Four
ORGANIZER

*M*y first official job with the IWW was as literature agent
out of Kamloops, British Columbia, over eighty miles
of construction camps of the Canadian Northern Railroad.
I would start from Lytton with seventy-five to eighty pounds
of *Solidarity* and the *Industrial Worker*—the Wobbly newspapers—as well as pamphlets, dues stamps, application
blanks, and red song books. I had to hike from camp to camp
where I would be welcomed by the members on the job and
taken to the mess hall where I was never charged for my
meals. In the evening I would lay out my wares on the table
in the largest bunkhouse and sell the papers and pamphlets,
collect dues from old members, and line up new ones. Next
morning, away to the next stop and the small contractors'
camps in between. There were a lot of these, and each one
would lighten my pack a little more. It took over six days
to make the last camp in my district. Then I would go over
to Kamloops, pick up the latest papers, and head back. I did
this for almost four months.

I was on one of these trips, just two days out of Lytton,
when the strike began. While walking to the next camp, I
met up with a small army of men—cooks, flunkies, crane
operators and laborers. "The strike is on!" they said. "Some
of the men are pulling them out up the other way." I turned
around and we pulled out the next camp which was ready
for us. News of this sort has a strange way of traveling on
ahead. On to Lytton where a meeting was called at once and
a strike committee organized.

I was still held on as literature agent, but had no hiking
to do further than two blocks uptown where I always sold
out my papers and pamphlets.

For the first month of the strike there was no trouble. The construction was tied up about ninety-nine percent, there being only a man here and there feeding and taking care of the horses in the camps that had them. We had our own mess hall staffed by real cooks and bakers, our own "police force" to keep the hard-rock men in line, mostly Swedes, big men and strong as hell, but good union men all.

One night we received word that a trainload of scabs was to be found at a small way-station on the Canadian Pacific about eight miles from Lytton. Volunteers were called to hike up there and wait for the train and try to keep them from going to work. About eighteen or twenty of us started out walking the railroad tracks. About four miles out of Lytton there appeared on the track ahead two officers of the North-west Mounted Police, red coats and all. I was up with the first six or eight fellow workers. We walked up to within ten feet of these mounties when one of them spoke. "OK, boys," he said, "this is it. We have instructions that this is as far as you go."

"Why?" we asked.

"We don't know, boys," he said, "but our orders are that you don't go no further."

We sat down on the tracks and tried to talk our way around these fellows. All of us were there in a bunch and the moun-tie said, "Now in case there are any of you boys who have ideas about going into the bush and getting around us, let me show you." He blew a whistle and about fifteen or twenty red coats showed in the timber and brush alongside the tracks. There was no getting around these fellows. They told us if they couldn't arrest us, they would shoot us. He talked to us so matter-of-factly we knew he wasn't fooling. So there was nothing to do but take his advice which was to turn around and go back before someone got hurt. "You can bet your sweet life it won't be any of us," he said. We did just that and it was the wisest move we could have made, and as far as I could see, it was the only one.

It turned out that very few of the scabs had got off the train at the way-station because some fellow workers had boarded the train in Kamloops and had wised up the workers and most of them refused to get off at the stop and came right on into Lytton where they were taken to strike headquarters, fed and made welcome.

As time went on and lines were drawn more and more tightly and after quite a few of the strikers had left the country, it became necessary to centralize the forces and activities of the remaining few hundred. So a large camp was established on a small peninsula on the outskirts of Kamloops, rough but well laid out. We rented this neck of land which jutted out into the Fraser River at the mouth of the North Thompson which came into the Fraser at this point. Large outdoor ovens were built and the bakers made and sold the bread they baked and the money was used to buy other supplies for the camp.

When we learned that there were quite a few men working about one hundred miles up the North Thompson, I was asked by Tommy Whitehead to go with one other fellow worker to look over the situation. I agreed and next day left with a bed-roll and grub and fellow worker Dolgrin. It took us about six days to reach the last camp.

We went to the camp at night and talked to the men there. Only a handful. We told them there was a bunch of strikers on the way up the river to run everyone off. This, of course, was bunk, but it did succeed in getting two or three of them to collect their time and start down the trail. Of course they told the story at the next camp, so that Dolgrin and I never did find out how many men had been working because at each camp we learned that most had already quit, but there must have been a lot.

At any rate, we headed back, and when we arrived at the bridge we would have to cross to reach Kamloops, I told Dolgrin to wait while I had a look around. Sure enough, there were two Northwest Mounties on the bridge. I went back to Dolgrin and told him, and we went looking along the bank of the river for a dugout. There were only two ways to get to camp: Cross the bridge and be pinched, or find a dugout and row across. The Indians were always leaving their dugouts pulled up on the bank.

As we found out later, we would have been picked up even had we crossed the river in a boat because they had raided the camp just two days before and arrested everyone in it. They had mounties waiting there for us in camp and one mountie later told us they had picked up every dugout for twenty miles up the river.

"Well," I told Dolgrin, "I guess we'll just have to try and bluff it out. Maybe they don't know who we are." I said I would go first. I was stopped about half way across. The mountie said, "Where you coming from and where are you going?"

I said, "I just quit my job in camp No. Four and I'm going into town."

"Oh, you did? Well, let me see your time slip." I knew it. The one question I dreaded, a dead giveaway. He said, "We had your description since the first men began to come into town. Where is the other fellow, your pal?"

"Oh," I said, "he's coming."

He said, "You're damn right he is! This is the only way into town unless he wants to go all the way to Fort George, about four hundred miles up river." I looked around and there came Dolgrin. We waited and when he got there I pretended I didn't know him, but it didn't work. "Come on, boys," said the mountie, "there's a nice warm jail waiting for you."

And, by golly, there was. There were about sixty Wobblies from the camp and we were given a rousing welcome.

So you like mush? Not just plain old oatmeal mush, but juicy mush consisting of oatmeal, wheat, barley, and Christ knows what? Of course, I know mush is grand food with a little sugar and milk; but if you ever had to eat it for over four months with nothing to put on it but salt and pepper, you would no doubt hold the same opinon of it I have held for all these years. As a steady diet for humans, interspersed with only one boiled potato and a piece of fat meat once a week, leave me out.

A few days after being taken to jail, we were all lined up and marched to a long room where we were told we were to be tried. Hell, none of us even knew we had been charged, but in a moment we were to learn that in good old Canada they did things differently. Sitting at a table slightly above the level of the rest of the room was Kamiron Red; that's the name we gave him as we were marched before him one at a time.

"Name?" he would call.

We gave it, and he would wave his long skinny hand and we were moved on while the next fellow worker was marched before him. It took only a few minutes for the slow moving line of men to cross the room, stopping just long enough to have their names checked off a list. Then we were marched back to jail. Not a one of us knew what his sentence was, and I don't think any of us ever found out. The backbone of the strike was broken. Or was it?

The conditions which had brought on the strike underwent big changes; food, they said, was better, bunkhouses were cleaned up, and wages were raised. I wonder: Is a strike lost because those who fought to change conditions do not get to enjoy them? I think not. I think a strike is a part of the total struggle, and where it has forced better conditions which are enjoyed by other members of the working class, it cannot be called a defeat.

I spent almost five months in Kamloop's jail. One day while I was about to light a smoke, which was against the rules, a little punk of a jailer caught me. I was brought up to the office and given three days in the black hole. Now, a black hole can be just three days and nights in the dark, or, as at Kamloops, it can be three days and nights in a cell four feet by six feet with only a six-inch square opening in the door which was opened only when they brought you one-quarter of a loaf of bread and one pint of water ever twenty-four hours. The air gets stale until you get down on the floor where it is not as bad. You have a bucket for your needs emptied each twenty-four hours. You get used to the smell about the second day. The days are hot, as the hole is near the furnace. At night it gets twice as cold as it was hot. You have no blankets. Sleep, if you can, is your best out. Some of the boys smuggled three cigarets inside the loaf of bread and three Chinese matches for me. I lit one of them and for the next twelve hours damn near suffocated.

Tommy Whitehead was put in this hole for three days and came out almost totally blind. They had to turn him loose so he could receive treatment at once. Good old Kamloops jail, full of pimps, gunmen and murderers, but the black hole was for the strikers.

I had written home while in jail, and one day I received a letter from Paterson, New Jersey, telling me my Dad was in Washington at my brother's place in Wilbur. One morning, not long after this, my name was called out and I was told to get ready. I was released.

I left the jail about nine a.m. and was met outside by a fellow worker who took me to a small office where the IWW was still in business in Kamloops. They gave me a fine meal and a ticket to Seattle. I left on the next train for Vancouver. I was to take the boat for Seattle, but when I went to be cleared in customs, the agent there would not let me board the ship. The American immigration officer said, ''You're not an American. I can see Canada sticking out all over you.'' I told him he was crazy. ''What railroads run through Paterson, New Jersey?'' he asked.

I told him the Erie, the DL&W and the Susquehanna. He said he never hear of the Susquehanna. I told him I didn't think he had as this little road only ran about fifty miles from Paterson and back. After about five or six hours another officer came on duty, and the one who wouldn't let me on the boat told him I was trying to pull a fast one. They left me there while they went into a small office. After a while the one who had just come on duty came back and said, ''OK, get aboard. We found out there is a railroad by that name in Paterson.''

I arrived in Seattle the next day, went to the Hall and saw Tommy Whitehead. Told him I was going to grab a freight for Spokane and go down to Wilbur to see my Dad.

Which I did. I arrived in Wilbur broke and dirty and found my Dad running a small lunch-counter in the rear of a large pool-hall. I had a good meal. When Dad said, ''Why don't you stay here a while and help me with the restaurant?,'' I agreed on a fifty-fifty basis. So for all that summer I cooked in this place. After the harvest, Dad began to show unmistakable signs of homesickness, and he was not feeling any too well.

I said, ''Dad, I think you should go home.''

He agreed at once, but said, ''Why don't you come with me?''

I hated like hell to put out the money, one hundred forty dollars each, but Dad didn't look too good, so I agreed. ''Let's split what we made and go down and get our tickets.''

I sold everything that I figgered belonged to Dad and me in the lunch room, and the next day, saying goodbye to my brother Ed, we left Wilbur for Spokane. We had to wait there until next morning for a train east, so I took Dad to a Wobbly street meeting and then to the hall where I said, ''Dad, how about signing up?'' To my surprise Dad did not protest. He signed an application and paid six months dues and became a member of the Industrial Workers of the World. Next morning we boarded the train for Paterson.

I was glad I had decided to see Dad home, for on the way he became very sick and I had to take care of him. He got better before we arrived home about five days later.

I found that the IWW was also active in Paterson. The Paterson silk strike of 1913 was two days old when we arrived. I attended a large meeting that very night at Turner Hall, where Gurley Flynn and W. D. Haywood spoke. They asked for people in the crowd to express their opinions on the strike. After some time when no one asked for the floor,

I stood up and called, "Mr. Chairman." He recognized me and I spoke, bringing them greetings from the strikers on the Canadian Northern and the men still in jail in British Columbia. Shortly after I spoke, a young fellow came up to me and told me the secretary of the local IWW would like to see me next morning. So the next day I went to see fellow worker Lessic, the local's secretary and chairman of the strike committee. He asked me if I was free and if I would work for the strike committee. I told him I would.

My first job was to try and pull out the Passaic, New Jersey, dye-houses which were hanging tough. I was given the men to work with me. We had four thousand leaflets printed with the wage demands and an appeal to the dye-house workers to join the strike.

We took the streetcar to within two blocks of the plant, and then we made our big mistake. We got off the streetcar and walked toward the plant all together. About one block away a large car drew up to the curb and five or six men jumped out. Before we knew what was going on, they had snatched the handbills from all three of the others. The fellow that came after me had both his hands on my bundle of leaflets. I held on for dear life. I was not going to let him get away with that, I thought, but one of the other plug-uglies came up behind me and before I knew what was happening, he pulled my coat over my head from behind. This, I learned later, was a trick they used to make a person helpless, and it sure worked. I lost my handbills. Giving me a shove which sent me staggering into a building, they jumped in their car and drove off. But we did get their number.

We went to the police station and said we wanted to make a holdup complaint. We gave the license number, but the cops just laughed at us and told us that our car was registered to the Burns Detective Agency and that the car and the men in it were never near where we were held up.

I told the other fellows to go back to Paterson. I would stay on and see what could be done. I went to an address I had gotten from Lessic and found an Italian family. I talked to the husband who was a dye house worker. He told me I could board with them. I asked him to get me as many addresses of his fellow workers as he could. At night I would go to these addresses and talk to the workers and leave them a leaflet. I must have gotten out three or four hundred leaflets that way when they began to talk strike at the plant. They were bringing the leaflets to work with them. One night we decided to try and pull them out the next day. We did. Within two days there were so few left that the plant had to close.

I went back to Paterson and reported to Lessic. He was pleased and asked me to go to Allentown, Pennsylvania, where there was one of the largest dye-works in the silk industry. Of course I went. The fellow worker who was sent with me and I found a very hard nut to crack, indeed. We couldn't get within two blocks of the plant because the police were stationed at all approaches to it. We passed out leaflets in the working class part of town with no way of knowing how many got into the right hands. We rented a hall and called a meeting, but the newspapers would not take our ads.

The fellow worker with me was a booze hound, and when I needed him most, I could never find him. One day I put about five hundred leaflets under my coat, picked up a lunch bucket, and when they began to change shifts, I got to the main gate. I started to put out leaflets right and left. The cops down on the corner from the gate didn't get wise until a fellow came rushing out of the gate and started to yell for the cops. They came running. I just kept passing out handbills until they grabbed me, pushed me into a police car and started uptown. Christ, you would have thought they caught America's Number One enemy! Well, I thought, here's where I get at least thirty days. But I underestimated the wise Allentown police.

When they brought me in, the chief said, "Don't book him, for Christ sake! Don't you know that's just what they want? First thing you know, they will have a bunch of lawyers up here and will get all the publicity they want. Just turn

"On the Road"— photograph by Saffo, illustrating Henry McGuckin's article, "An Old-Timer," in the August 1914 issue of the *International Socialist Review*

him loose and make sure he don't get near that dye-house again.''

I went back to Paterson and reported to the strike committee on Allentown. Lessic said we would try something else. "Stick around Paterson for a while and keep in touch with me," he said.

I helped with the meetings at Turner Hall and went on the picketline. One day they had beat up and arrested a lot of pickets. I was standing across the street from the patrol cars when a big cop, whom I at once recognized, began to disperse the crowd. About six foot four, two hundred fifty pounds of dumb flesh and bone. I watched him clout several people and clear the sidewalk. This was the same son of a bitch who damn near made me deaf and broke the lobes of my ears when he was truant officer. Duck-foot Farlon, we kids used to call him. Big, tough, and ignorant. He didn't recognize me.

I stayed in Paterson only a week or two longer as I wanted to get back out west. I told my Dad goodbye and jumped a freight heading for the wide open spaces. After an uneventful trip I landed in St. Paul, Minnesota, where the streetcar conductors were on strike.

It was in St. Paul that I made my first real speech on a soapbox, the first of many hundreds of such talks, in many places and in many states. I was standing in the crowd listening to the soapboxer when a fellow worker started to talk to me. Of course, the question was always, "Where did you blow in from?"

I told him, "Paterson."

"Was you in the strike?"

"Yes," I said, "I did some work for the strike committee."

"You got to tell the crowd about that," he said.

I said, "Hey, I can't get up there."

"The hell you can't. Your're a Wobbly, ain't you?"

"Sure. What's that got to do with it?"

"Any Wobbly that has strike news," he said, "has got to tell about it. You're going to get up on that box and talk.

Don't be afraid. I'll be right behind you."

I wondered what the hell good that was going to do. Being right behind me wouldn't put words into my mouth.

But he pulled me over to the speaker and said, "Hey, here's a fellow worker just in from Paterson, New Jersey. The silk strike. Let him up there."

The soapboxer got down and with the help of Kline, the fellow worker who insisted I speak, I was pushed up on the box. "Fellow workers," I shouted, trying to be heard over the din of streetcars, "I want to tell you about the Paterson strike. The silk workers are all on strike back there."

Kline pulled my coat and said, "They know that! Tell them just what you saw—the picketlines, the cops, the beatings, the meetings."

So I tried, and after a few moments of stuttering and searching, the words began to fall into place. After all, there was a lot to talk about when you had seen 25,000 strikers in action.

After I was through, Kline jumped up on the soapbox and took up a collection for strikers. Pretty good, too, as I remember—fifteen or sixteen dollars. We took the money up to the hall, where the transport workers had finished their closed meeting, and turned it over to the secretary. I had to speak all over again to the streetcar men who had been in the hall while the street meeting was going on.

I left St. Paul and headed for the coast, working the hayfields of Dakota, Montana, Idaho. Again in Seattle, I ran into a couple of hard rock Swedes I had known during the Canadian Northern strike. They insisted I stay with them while they tried to drink all the beer and whiskey in Seattle. I went around with them for a few days when one of them said, "Let's go to California."

I had wanted to go there, so I said, "Sure. Let's go!"

Well, the Swedes headed for the docks where they paid for three tickets to Stockton, California. We sailed next morning. After an uneventful trip we arrived in Stockton where I located the IWW hall and met Jimmy Roheu. That night I spoke with Roheu on the Stockton square. A few nights later the police stopped us from speaking in Stockton. This proved to be about as short a free speech fight as I know of.

About fifteen or twenty of us were thrown in jail that night. We were put in the tank on the top floor of the courthouse. From the moment we were locked up until we were released, we gave the courthouse no rest. We built a "battleship," using the tin plates, cups and whatever we could pry loose. The noise was terrific. They couldn't hold court. Office workers on the floors below couldn't work. The sheriff who lived in the building couldn't get any sleep. They threatened and swore and turned the fire hoses on us. We barricaded with mattresses against the water and the "battleship" went on.

On the morning of the third day they came in. "OK, boys!" they yelled, "Cut it out now. We're turning you out." They did, and that night Roheu and I again spoke at the Stockton square.

I also spent a lot of time speaking in Oakland, Richmond and San Francisco, making a trip now and again to Fresno and Bakersfield. It was during this time that the strike in the hop fields began. On August 2, 1913, the police tried to break up a peaceful meeting of the hop-pickers at the Durst Ranch and, led by deputy sheriff Dirkin, they started using their guns on the strikers. Someone with a gun fired back and killed both Dirkin and the district attorney. They of course arrested the leaders in the strike, Ford and Suhr.

I went to Stockton at once where we held meeting after meeting, raising money for their defense. Then back again to Oakland and more meetings for Ford and Suhr. At the IWW hall one day, Austin Lewis, who was the defense attorney, asked that some sort of plan be worked out whereby a number of well-behaved fellow workers could be stationed in Marysville, where the trial was held, to show the people there that the Wobblies weren't a bunch of cut-throats and criminals. I was one of about twenty chosen to go. We rented a two-story house in a good part of town. We found the public library where eight or twelve of us were to be found for most of the opening hours. The others attended the trial and spoke quietly, and all in all, we were a very model group of hard-reading, well-behaved young men. A reporter from one of the local newspapers wrote a story about the young men who were freqenting the public library, reading books that had been uncalled for years, requesting others that the library did not have, and about the orderly group of young men of the IWW who attended the trial each day. Just how much good this did I'm not able to say. Let it be said, however, that whereas before they had been trying to hang Ford and Suhr, the special prosecutor they brought in for the trial did not ask for the death penalty but for life imprisonment. This was a complete switch and may or may not been influenced by our group in town.

But I am firmly convinced that it was not a result of Austin Lewis' speech to the jury—a long, drawn-out explanation of the class struggle and solidarity, which I am sure did not interest that jury in the least. The local attorney who was hired to help Lewis pinned down the evidence in such a way as to force the prosecution into asking for a lesser verdict. To my mind he proved that Ford and Suhr had no part in the shooting, and he did it so well that the special prosecutor asked for a recess at once. After about an hour, he came back into court and made his final statement to jury, asking for a life sentence.

We Wobblies were not surprised when the jury returned a verdict of guilty and endorsed the life sentence. Such were the farmers of those days. Interfere with the crops, strike against the low wages and the rotten conditions under which their workers lived, and they were ready to hang, lynch, tar and feather anyone in sight. If it happened to be a Wobbly, all the better.

After the trial I returned to San Francisco where George Speed was secretary of the local. It was here I met fellow worker Lone Wolf. I never knew his right name. He was, I suppose, to some who didn't know him, a very ugly person. He had a bullet-shaped head that sat on a long neck, large eyes that stood out so far you would wonder why they didn't fall out completely, and very big nose and mouth. But that was as far as Lone Wolf's ugliness went. He was mild, intelligent, and very kind. I grew to like him very much. He wasn't easy to know, and if he thought your interest was just out of pity, he avoided you from then on. But with me it wasn't pity, and he seemed to know this and became a fine friend. When he got in a disagreement with some fellow workers, he would call me over and say, "Hey Mac! Ain't that right?" Even before I knew the question. He seemed to think I knew all the answers, and sometimes I had quite a problem getting both of us out of some screwy argument which I had no part in starting.

I went over to Oakland to speak for the local there for a while. Lone Wolf followed the next month. Here I met another character who could get you killed or beaten up if you weren't on your guard: Smokey Jones. Now Smokey was a fairly good soapboxer under certain conditions—when there was no cop within hearing or sight. But let one appear and Smokey could not resist dropping everything else. He would say, "Ah! There he comes! There is the cause of all our troubles! Look at him! The big, fat, pussy-faced, whiskey-bloated savage!" This, despite the fact the cop would sometimes not be overly large, but about the size and complexion of forty or fifty other people in the crowd.

Smokey hated cops, but not for the reason that criminals hate cops. He could see in them all the brutality, the clubbings and jailings that had been and were being heaped upon the working class. When we would tell him he had to stop that stuff on that soapbox, he would shout, "Hell, you fellows never will see! Can't you understand? Get rid of the cops and the revolution will be tomorrow!" From the clubbings and beatings Smokey had taken in free-speech fight after free-speech fight, from railroad bulls and vigilantes, they were all cops to him, and the success or failure of the class war depended upon getting rid of them.

Smokey disappeared one day and I never found out from anyone where he had gone or what had happened to him. I met no one who ever saw him again. I heard talk of his being beaten to death, of his falling under a freight, and so on, but knowing Smokey, I believe the first is more likely to be true.

It was about this time in the hall on Tenth Street in Oakland that I was to meet and work with John Panzner. We were concentrating at that time on organizing the oil refinery workers and dock workers at Richmond, California. John and I spoke there afternoons and evenings with some degree of success. John was a real organizer, a charter member of the IWW from the very beginning, a farmer and a socialist and a fine speaker, calm and never excited when trouble was brewing. But in an argument with a group of fellow workers, he could be as loud and as mad as anyone I had ever seen. If he was extremely interested in a tactic and couldn't make them see it right off, John would give them hell as a lot of "spittoon philosophers." I never disagreed much with John. As a rule I would find out he was right more often than not.

MORE WAGES
BETTER WORKING CONDITIONS
SHORTER HOURS
EMANCIPATION
W·I·W
SOLIDARITY
ABOLITION -- WAGE SYSTEM
ABOLITION OF UNEMPLOYMENT
SHOP DEMOCRACY
GOOD PAY OR BUM WORK

THINK IT OVER
JOIN THE
ONE BIG UNION
FIGHT FOR THE FULL PRODUCT
OF YOUR LABOR

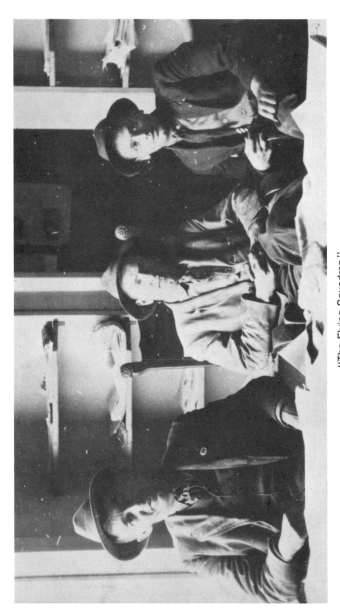

"The Flying Squadron."
Left to right: John Panzner, Saffo, Henry McGuckin

Five

The Flying Squadron

*T*he trip of the Flying Squadron began in Oakland in 1913, at the IWW hall. I was nineteen years old at the time.

Panzner, who had been in Nevada some years before in the heyday of the Western Federation of Miners, and when the IWW had Goldfield and Tonapah well organized among the culinary workers, wanted to go back and see how things were on his old stamping grounds. He asked me if I wanted to go along. I agreed. Saffo, a college kid from New York, asked if he could go and we took him along.

We went to the yards and took a freight headed for Truckee, California. We had little or no money, but figured on soapboxing and selling literature to make enough to eat. As for sleeping, we would sleep where we could. We arrived late in the afternoon at Truckee and got off the freight just before it went into the snowsheds. Walking along the tracks to town, we ran into a sight that stopped us cold.

There was a windbreak of railroad ties stacked up in a half-diamond shape alongside the tracks. A small fire was burning in the center of the windbreak, and huddled in the corner of the half diamond was the figure of a man. When we approached we found an old man of about sixty-five sitting on an old box, a torn piece of blanket around his shoulders, his frozen feet wrapped in many folds of gunny sacks. An old can was stewing on the coals of the fire. It had coffee in it. He said he had used the same grounds three times. It was nothing but colored water.

We talked to him for most of the night. He told us he was an old construction worker. He had helped build railroads, dams, and roads all over the west and southwest, but he couldn't work anymore. He had rheumatism so bad his joints were all swollen and stiff. His old hands were all bent and curled, hard as nails from axe and saw, pick and shovel.

He had tried to get help from county hospitals and poor farms, but because he had no place he could call home he was always turned away. He had been there in that wind-break for over a month. Passing hobos would give him a little grub at times, some bread and coffee. They would get wood and pile it close to keep the fire going. But for the help of the passing hobos he would have died there. We got him some grub, wood and water, and then Saffo, who had a camera along, took some pictures and developed them in the open that same night. I wrote the old man's story and called it: "On the Scrap Heap."

Saffo, when he read it the next day, wanted to change it. I told him, "You go back to your college and you write the story any way you like, but this little story is going to the *International Socialist Review*. Just like this. Just as he told it, plain and simple, and no one is going to murder it with a lot of big words that the old man didn't use and probably never even heard." It went off that way with the pictures. It came out in the August, 1914 issue with the title "An Old Timer." Not a word was changed, not one added nor taken out. We had signed it with no names, just The Flying Squadron.

Mary E. Marcy at the Charles H. Kerr Company, Chicago paid us by sending one hundred copies of the *Review* when we were in Reno, Nevada. This was ten dollars, as they sold for ten cents a copy.

Leaving Truckee we went on to Reno where Saffo left us and Panzner and I held some meetings. We didn't stay long in Reno, but left on foot and walked across country to Virginia City, then a real ghost town.

We rested up there and then took off across country again headed for Rawhide. I can remember it was a long, dusty, hot walk along roads that were only ruts in the sand. The

AUGUST, 1914   *The*   PRICE TEN CENTS

INTERNATIONAL SOCIALIST REVIEW

"HE BUILT THE ROAD"

Articles by

Phillips Russell	William D. Haywood	Frank Bohn
Emile Pouget	Charles Edw. Russell	Eugene V. Debs

This issue of the *International Socialist Review*
included Henry McGuckin's article, "An Old-Timer"
(August 1914)

water was brackish and alkaline in the only water hole we came to on the way.

When we arrived in Rawhide we found some old-time union men still there. Only one saloon was left in the almost deserted gold town. About a hundred or so people remained out of what had been ten or twelve thousand. The saloon was a real western type with a long bar, about half a hundred feet or so. We held a meeting that night in the bar and just about every miner in Rawhide was there. We sold our copies of the *International Socialist Review*, the *Industrial Worker* and *Solidarity*, and various pamphlets—Jack London's *Strength of the Strong; The Right to be Lazy; Socialism, Utopian and Scientific*, and others. The collection and sale of papers and pamphlets was very good.

The next day we walked to the railroad and jumped a freight for Tonapah. We rented a shack, brought some grub, and cleaned up from our trip.

That night we held our first street meeting and were well received. I would start the meeting with a song and then speak a little while and introduce Panzner who was a good organizer. He knew his industrial unionism and could explain it in simple, understandable terms. Our nightly meetings grew bigger and bigger as time passed, and Panzner became busy organizing the hotel and restaurant workers. In just a few weeks a charter was issued by the national office at Chicago. Panzner rented the Western Federation of Miners hall as an office and meeting place.

It was only a few weeks after they were organized that the hotel and restaurant workers gained increased wages, and we began a drive to organize the other culinary workers in town.

The large boarding houses were at that time a large part of the industry in mining towns, and there was one boarding house that held out, Mrs. Harrington's. It employed a number of kitchen workers and waiters. John Panzner began carrying a sign out front stating that Mrs. Harrington was unfair to organized labor. Some miners, mostly Irish who owed

Mrs. Harrington board money, came down to bust up the union hall. I was in Goldfield that night holding some street meetings, and when I got back to Tonopah next day, Panzner was in jail, charged with shooting one of the miners in the foot. They had tried to get up to the office to destroy the records. Panzner told them to stay where they were. They rushed at him, and he fired, hitting one of them in the foot.

How he hit anyone with that gun I shall never know. It was a small .32 caliber pistol with a broken mainspring. I fixed it by putting the handle of a soup spoon in as a spring. I could not pull the trigger after that except by holding it in both hands and squeezing with all my might. I asked Panzner how in hell he fired that gun and hit anyone, and he said he just pulled the trigger. But you can tell how hard it must have been when he fired at a man at close range and only hit him in the foot.

I began at once to organize a defense and for the next month or six weeks was very busy. I got a woman we both knew there, Minnie Abbott, to act as treasurer and began to send out hundreds of letters for funds. We wired Fred Moore, a lawyer in Los Angeles, to defend John, and I must say this was a mistake. Not that Fred Moore was not a good lawyer, but a common mistake made by the IWW was in hiring outside lawyers to defend our members.

It had been my experience that a good local lawyer can do much better and is less costly and, in labor cases, you stand a much better chance of getting your man off. You don't need to fight the prejudice engendered in the local law circles by bringing in outside talent. This was proven by the Ford and Suhr case where we had an outside lawyer, and, had it not been for the local lawyer who was also brought in on the case, Ford and Suhr would have hung. Also it proved wiser in the Mesabi Range cases of Scarlett, Tresca and Smith, who, thanks to the local lawyers brought into the case, were never even brought to trial.

Anyway, Panzner was sent to prison for a year, and I was left alone in Tonopah. I continued to hold street meetings and lived from hand to mouth for some time. About a month or more after Panzner went to jail, the cops stopped my street meetings. I was the only speaker there so I couldn't very well fill the jail myself. I sent out a call to the organization to send in some free-speech fighters and about ten or so arrived in the following weeks.

We decided to hold a meeting, but the law had its own ideas about filling their jail. Instead, they let us speak a little while and then, as the others tried to follow me, they were beaten up by the cops and the group of thugs they had with them. I was pulled out of the crowd by a special cop who always seemed to want to protect me. He said, "Come on, you damn fool kid!" He hurried me along and locked me in a little jail they kept for drunks and those they just wanted to lock up for the night. He locked me up in spite of my protests and said, "I'll let you out in the morning."

Next morning I went to the shack where the rest of the Wobblies were. Some had black eyes, but no one was hurt bad. Well, here was a new tactic to contend with.

After some discussion, we decided that the street meetings were not important enough to get hurt real bad, so we put off further action for the time being. A few days later, Jack Whyte came to Tonopah and since Jack was a good speaker, we began to hold meetings in the miners' hall.

It was during this time that the cops began to try harder to discourage me and get me to leave town. They pinched me for vagrancy and took me before a Socialist justice of the peace. I was turned loose on my own recognition, and I came to trial, acting as my own attorney. After having a lot of fun with the county attorney, I laid out a bunch of receipts from Minnie Abbott for eighteen dollars a week as a member of the Panzner Defense Committee. Hell, I never received a nickel from that fund. The district attorney said he knew I was a damn liar. "But Abbott will swear she paid you that money, so you win this round!"

The district attorney was running for re-election about then against a Socialist lawyer who, through Jack Whyte, got in touch with me. He gave me twenty-five dollars and about one hundred cards with the county attorney's name on them. Now I was well known as no friend of the district attorney's so when I began to buy a round of drinks for the boys in the saloons and to pass out his cards, you can figure what happened—the whole town was laughing. The district attorney found me in the big casino about six o'clock that night. The chief of police and two deputies were with him. Well, they grabbed me and hustled me out to the street where a big crowd had formed. Everyone came out of the saloon and while the two deputies held me, the D.A. was shouting, "Tell them! Tell them who put you up to this!"

I said, "Why, we talked it over this morning, don't you remember?"

He said, "You're a damn liar! I wouldn't be seen dead with you!"

The crowd was busting its sides with laughter when one of the deputies slammed me in the jaw. I kept shouting, "That's a hell of a way to treat a friend!"

Then the same cop who saved me from a beating before came through the crowd and, pushing the other cops aside, said, "Let me have him. He's only a kid and he's got more guts than all of you."

He took me out of there and locked me up in the same jail and told me that was the last time. If I got in any more trouble, I could get out of it myself. He said, "You keep this up, you're sure as hell going to get yourself killed."

A few days later there was an explosion at the office of the *Tonopah Bonanza*, the town's only newspaper, owned and edited by a man named Booth. Next day the paper came out with large headlines saying "*Bonanza* Blown Up." Then a detailed report of what happened. It stated that a mass meeting would be held that night at which Booth would name those responsible.

That night in a large meeting hall, the meeting was held. Booth was introduced and proceeded to blame the IWW, the Socialists, and everyone else he didn't agree with. Now that afternoon I had gone to the newspaper building and looked at the damage. When Booth got through talking, I asked for the floor. After a lot of shouting, ''Throw him out!'' ''Let him speak!'' and so on, I finally got the platform, and I told them I had looked over the damage the blast had done, and I could assure them that no one who wanted to cause much damage had planted the dynamite. It looked like an inside job to me. I said anyone who knew anything about dynamite would never just put a stick of it under the corner of the building and light the fuse, as must have been done here. Since all the Wobblies and Socialists were miners or knew about mining, it couldn't have been them, but maybe a newspaper editor could have done it to get attention, because whoever did it sure didn't want to cause any damage.

Well, Booth jumped up and rushed toward me. He yelled, ''You accusing me of blowing up my own paper?''

I told him I was almost sure of it. The crowd was yelling, but most of them were laughing. The laughter was so contagious the meeting had to break up. Next day not a word in the paper about the dynamiting or the meeting.

A few days later we held a large meeting in an old showhouse, a large place that held about five hundred people. I do not remember who the speaker was, but I know it was someone speaking for the Socialist Party. About an hour after the meeting was over the hall caught fire. Needless to say, on old frame building like that burned to the ground. A few days later the chief of police, through the paper, blamed the IWW for the fire. They questioned Whyte and Abbott, who it seems had an alibi. Then they questioned me. I couldn't prove just where I was after this meeting was over. I knew where I was but no one came forward to uphold my statement that I was blocks away when the fire started.

I was arrested by Police Chief Evans and lodged in the county jail after a hearing before the Socialist Justice of the Peace who had always been kind to me. He said, ''This time, Mac, I can't turn you loose unless you have an alibi.'' I told him I didn't even believe in the kind of sabotage that endangered lives, but that I understood he couldn't do anything else.

So for almost three months I was held in jail, waiting for the grand jury to act. When they did, I was turned loose for lack of evidence, pending, as they put it, further investigation. While I was waiting for them to act, they had arrested and convicted a young Wobbly and gave him twenty years.

After I was released from jail, I just rested for a few days and enjoyed being out of jail. One night Jack White, Minnie Abbott, and myself had finished closing out the final accounting of the John Panzer Defense Fund at Minnie's cabin. We were sitting around just talking when there was a crash against the door. White jumped up and grabbed a miner's pick. Abbott grabbed a small gun. The second crash broke down the door, and a gambler named Stegal burst into the room carrying a .45 pistol. White threw the miner's pick and missed. Abbott just screamed and dropped the pistol she held. White closed with Stegal, and as he did I heard a shot. White fell on the floor. Stegal looked at me once—I wasn't five feet from him—then ran out of the shack.

I stood there looking at White, trying to figure out what in hell it was all about. I still don't know to this day why Stegal, a gambler and no Wobbly, shot Jack White—a woman problem, I think.

White was conscious. He looked at me and said, ''I can't move my legs.'' I ran out to get a doctor. I was gone only a few moments. I came back and waited for the doctor who arrived with the police. He examined White and told us the bullet had cut the spinal cord. We had White taken to the county hospital where he was to stay until I could get him moved to San Francisco.

The day after the shooting, White asked Abbott and me to see him. We went to the hospital and Jack said, as a favor to him, not to say anything in court the next day since he was not going to prosecute. Well, of course, it was up to him, and at the hearing the next day we refused to say anything about the shooting, and Stegal was turned loose.

White was never going to get well. I knew that, and so did he. So when Abbott went to San Francisco, I told her to get in touch with some of Jack's old friends. In about a week I received word that a Joe Hansen and Oliver Twitmore of the San Francisco Labor Council had reserved a room at McNutt's Hospital for White, but the question was how was I to get him there? I went to the hospital and told White. I told him I thought I had a way to get him there, and he told me to go ahead.

That morning I went into the biggest gambling hall in Tonopah and looked up the houseman. I told him I wanted to talk to some of Stegal's friends. I said, "I either talk to them or I talk to the D.A." I would not keep quiet any longer and let White die alone in that county hospital.

He took me into a back room and in a few minutes four or five of Tonopah's leading gamblers came in. They said, "What's on your mind, kid?" I told them White had a room reserved for him in a hospital at San Francisco, but he had to have railroad fare, a nurse and a pullman drawing room, and if they were not forthcoming, I was going to tell what I saw, whether White wanted to prosecute or not.

Well, about two o'clock in the afternoon I was stopped on the street by a man I knew as a gambler. He said, "OK, kid. Have White at the train tomorrow morning. We'll have everything ready."

The next morning the ambulance brought White to the train. They put him aboard and just before the train pulled out, the houseman I had first contacted came over to me and said, "Mac, we decided that we would buy one for you, too. Unless you get on that train and go along with White, the whole deal's off." I accepted, and, in fact, if they hadn't bought me a ticket, I would have caught the next freight train out of there anyway, for I could do no more in Tonopah. So ended the trip of the Flying Squadron. White died in San Francisco a few months later and was given a rebel's funeral by the IWW.

Six

THE LAST YEARS

I did not attend the funeral of Jack White. At the time he died, April, 1915, I was on my way as a delegate from the Oakland local of th IWW to a meeting in Kansas City, Missouri, to formulate plans to organize the agriculture workers.

Jack Law, Ted Frazer and I left together and went up to Stockton where we held several meetings to raise money for an appeal for Ford and Suhr. We knew a few men who worked in the yards of the Western Pacific. We asked them to check the next fast freight and find a car billed to Kansas City. They found one and gave us the number of the car. That night we went to the yards and looked up the car. There were a couple of fellow workers with us to see us off. We sprang the door on the car and climbed in. We were lucky as it was a load of sacked wool and we knew the trip would be warm. We had a little food and some water, which did not last too long, but it turned out we went without water only two days since this car was taken from one division to the other very rapidly. Wool is dangerous and they move it fast to prevent spontaneous combustion.

We arrived in Kansas City and, calling out, had a hobo break the seal and open the door. We made for the first restaurant we could find, and as we had a few dollars, we ate a good meal.

The next day we met at ten a.m. in the IWW hall in Kansas City. There were nine delegates present: myself, Ted Frazer, Jack Law, Albert Prashner, a fellow named Christ, G.J. Berg, and three others whose names I can't remember. We met for three days and formulated a tentative plan of organization for the harvest fields for that summer. We elected Walter T. Nef, who was then in Philadelphia, secretary-treasurer. He came to Kansas City the next week. It was decided that the headquarters of what we had named the Agricultural Workers Organization, IWW, later to be better known as Local 400, was to be in Minneapolis, Minnesota, so as to be near the center of harvest activities.

Through the hard work and the know-how of Nef, our effort to organize—for the first time in the history of this country—the agricultural and migratory workers was to meet with great success in the short space of only two years. We began with nine members and reached more than one hundred thousand! The AWO was so successful that the government of this country was brought into the picture, and using the excuse of the first world war, decided that this radical organization would be smashed once and for all.

For one thing, we solved the problem of organizing the unorganized. As a start, we had what was known as the speakers' circuit: Jack Law, Albert Prashner, Arthur Boose, Ted Frazer, Charles Ashleigh, and myself. We would speak once a week at a town and then be replaced by others on the circuit—Minneapolis, St. Paul, Sioux City, Kansas City, Des Moines, and so on. We held meetings in towns that had never had street meetings before except by the Salvation Army. We ran into some interesting situations—sometimes kind of amusing, sometimes not so.

I remember one night when we were in Wichita, Kansas, I was on the soap box. We had a very large crowd when the cops came along. Neither Frazer, Law nor myself knew anything about Wichita. Nor did we know anyone there. But when the cops started to push their way through the crowd, the crowd or most of them began to push back. One man got in front of me and said, "Just what in hell do you fellows think you're doing?" One of the cops tried to explain that they didn't want the IWW around, and they were going to stop the meeting. I just stood on the box taking it all in. A fellow who turned out to be the secretary of the Socialist Party, which was strong in Wichita, told him, "You stop this meeting and you're through in Wichita! Who the hell do you think you are, telling people what they can listen to? Now you take your cops and do the job you were elected to do, and don't try to stop this meeting because if you do, I'll take over and hold this meeting under the auspices of the Socialist Party and invite these boys to speak.'' The cops left.

We stayed there a week at the insistence of the Socialist Party. When we ran out of IWW literature, we sold Socialist Party pamphlets and the *Appeal to Reason*. Well, we spoke through Oklahoma, Montana, and Idaho. In Idaho we traveled by way of the Silver Dollar route. This route was so named because the train crews demanded one dollar from all those riding the trains across the desolate few hundred miles between Butte and Pocatello. ''Hungry-man land'' it was called. Law, Frazer, and I were kicked off our freight about forty miles out of Pocatello. We had refused to put up the dollar. We got off at a water tank and in about two days there were ten or twelve Wobblies at this tank.

One night we decided to take the front end of the night passenger. I thought at the time there were a few too many of us, but we made about ten miles before the train slowed down and the conductor, a very hard-boiled customer, put us off. As the train started up again, we all climbed back on. We only went about a mile when the same thing happened. He told us the next time someone was going to get hurt.We climbed back on as it pulled out, and in not over five minutes, the door was flung open and out came ''hard-boiled,'' a big .45 in his hand. He fired a shot in the air and pulled the cord to stop the train. Frazer had cut the cord, however, and nothing happened. I could see this guy was crazy, so when Ted Frazer started going hand over hand out on the engine water-tender, I followed. For almost too long we hung there with our fingers clutching the edge of the tender, our bodies and legs whipped by the wind, hanging in space, and that train wasn't going less than sixty.

Well, most of the boys had jumped before the train reached top speed, and when the conductor sent his brakeman over the tender to stop the train, we dropped off. My arms were like sticks and my fingers flattened out like pancakes. I was skinned up, too. Ted Frazer was worse off than me and it was a long time before he could stand up and walk.

We sat there a while and waited until one by one the others came along. After a while we found them all accounted for and started down the track. We decided that the next freight was going to take us to Pocatello.

When it came along, we found an empty boxcar and dived in. Along came a couple of brakemen. "Come out of there, you goddamn bums! Get up your dollar!"

We went to the door of the boxcar and told them, "Look boys, we are all union men. We are riding this train to Pocatello, so you be good union men and forget it." Oh no, they were going to have their dollars or we didn't ride. "OK," we told them, "Come on in and put us off."

One of them made a jump for the door, and I saw he had a gun. I made a dive for him and shouted for Law to get the gun. He did, and then Law and I had a hell of a time keeping the other Wobblies from beating them. We told them to beat it before we beat the hell out of them. They did and when the train was within eight or ten miles of Pocatello, we boosted a fellow onto the roof, and going between the cars, he slowly cut the air off, slowing down the train until we were all off. Then he put the air back on and hopped off himself. We scattered and met Law and Frazer on the other side of Pocatello.

We drifted back east by easy stages and back to Minneapolis where after a week or two, another speakers' circuit was organized for which I was one of the speakers. This lasted for about five weeks of speaking in five different towns in the middle west. A week in each, then each man moved to the next town. This was the activity which built up the beginnings of Local 400 and was discontinued when the workers began to move to the fields. Then Nef put into being the delegate system which would to prove to be one of the greatest and fastest organization tactics, not surpassed to this day.

When the harvest began and the job delegates began to arrive in the fields, many men were organized in the hobo jungles while waiting for the wheat to ripen. As fast as they were issued a union card, many were at the same time issued job delegate credentials so that when the farmer hired his crew, there were always two or three job delegates among them. These job delegates could issue an IWW card right in the field, and did. I saw harvest workers organized and issued cards on freight trains, going from one part of the harvest fields to another, northwest, always northwest, from Kansas to Calgary, Alberta, Canada.

In the first year of the AWO, 1915, there were many problems that had to be overcome. The farmers were slow to accept unionism. This we knew; so our plan was to do a good job on the job. The first year we got the best wages we could, and the best hours. It wasn't long before the farmers saw that being able to hire a whole crew that was organized meant they could get their work done much faster than before when they had to run around looking for a crew.

There were beefs about wages, food, sleeping arrangements, and so on. They were mostly settled in favor of harvest workers because of the time element involved. The wheat was ripe. There was not much time to fight about it and since the workers did not make ridiculous demands, they were in most cases settled quickly.

There was one serious problem that had always been a nightmare for the harvest worker. This was the hi-jacker, the holdup man. There were many of them, and not all were plain holdup men. They were, and we proved it many times, the train crews on the freights that the harvest workers were riding. Yes, and the railroad dicks and the law in some of the towns in the harvest country. We had always known this to be a fact, but never before were we organized to do something about it. Some of the old-time Wobblies got together to talk it over. Only the most tested and time-proven

Wobs were involved, and this was never known to the membership of the organization as a whole.

Small units of not less than two or more than three were organized in such a way that each unit knew only itself, and while they knew there were others involved, they had no way of knowing who they were. Their purpose was to clean up the harvest fields of holdup men, whether they were parts of train crews, railroad detectives, law officers, or just plain holdup men. During the clean-up, freight trains might pull into their division points with a brakeman missing, never to be found. A railroad dick would be reported missing in the same way.

This might seem brutal to some, but when you have seen harvest workers thrown from freight trains at high speed, beaten up and robbed by small-town cops, shot by railroad dicks, whole groups of twenty to thirty held up at one time in a box car, then forced to jump off the train or be shot and thrown off—all of this over the years without recourse to any redress from the law or anyone else—you see only the need to stop it. That's what the Wobblies did.

When a member of the IWW named Schmidt shot and killed two holdup men in a boxcar full of harvest workers who had just been paid off and were moving farther north, he was tried for murder in Aberdeen and found not guilty by a jury of farmers. You can understand how bad these holdups had become—even the farmers knew about them. By the end of the second year of the AWO, holdups were few and far between.

The AWO did not stop with organizing the harvest workers. As the harvest workers left the fields, they found jobs in the lumber industry of the Northwest, on construction jobs in almost every state, in the mines, the mills, and on the waterfront, east, west, north, and south, after the harvest. The AWO organized them all, whatever the job.

* * *

After a short time as secretary of the branch in Kansas City, I headed for Chicago.

I was in Chicago in November, 1915, when we got word of Joe Hill's execution in Utah. Joe was the bard of the IWW, a gentle man who couldn't have committed the murder he was accused of. But they killed him anyway because he was a Wobbly and because his songs and poems were sharper than their swords. His last words were, "Don't mourn for me. Organize!" And he left this will:

> *My will is easy to decide,*
> *For there is nothing to divide.*
> *My kin don't need to fuss or moan—*
> *Moss does not cling to a rolling stone.*
>
> *My body? Ah! If I could choose,*
> *I would to ashes it reduce,*
> *And let the merry breezes blow*
> *My dust to where some flowers grow.*
>
> *Perhaps some fading flower then,*
> *Would come to life and bloom again.*
> *This is my last and final will,*
> *Good luck to all of you.*
> *—Joe Hill*

After speaking on Chicago street corners for a few weeks, I attended a night meeting and dance at which Big Bill Haywood spoke and where he called upon me to recite the "Dishwasher," a poem by Jim Seymour which was a favorite among the Wobs and about my best recitation. It went like this:

> *Alone in the kitchen, in a grease-laden steam*
> *I pause for a moment, a moment to dream,*
> *For even a dishwasher thinks of a day*
> *wherein will be leisure for rest and for play;*
> *And now that I pause o'er the transom there floats*
> *A stream of the Traumerei's soul-stirring notes,*

Engulfed in a blending of sorrow and glee
I wonder that music can reach even me.

For now I am thinking, my brain has been stirred,
The voice of a master the lowly has heard,
The heartbreaking sob of the sad violin
Arouses the thoughts of the sweet "might have been";
Had men been born equal the use of the brain
Would shield them from poverty, free them from pain,
Nor would I have sunk in the black social mire
Because of poor judgment in choosing a sire.

But now I am only a slave of the mill
That plies and remodels me just as it will,
That makes me a dullard in brain-burning heat
That looks at rich viands, not daring to eat;
That lives with its red, blistered hands ever stuck
Down deep in the foul indescribable muck
Where dishes are plunged, seventeen at a time,
And washed!—in a tubful of sickening slime!

But on with the clatter, no more must I shirk,
The world is to me but a nightmare of work;
For me not the music and laughter and song,
No toiler is welcomed amid the gay throng;
For me not the smiles of the ladies who dine,
No warm, clinging kisses begotten of wine;
For me but the venting of low, sweated groans
That twelve hours a night have installed in my bones.

The music has ceased, but the havoc it wrought
Within my poor brain it awakened to thought,
Shall cease not at all, but continue to spread
Till all of my fellows are thinking or dead.
The havoc it wrought? 'Twill be havoc to those
Whose joys would be nil were it not for my woes.
Keep on with your gorging, your laughter and jest,
But never forget that the last laugh is best.

You leeches who live on the fat of the land,
You overfed parasites, look at my hands;
You laugh at them now, they are blistered and coarse,
But such are the hands quite familiar with force;
And such are the hands that have furnished your drink,
The hands of the slaves who are learning to think,
And hands that have fed you can crush you as well
And cast your damned carcasses clear into hell!

Go on with the arrogance born of your gold,
As now are your hearts will your bodies be cold;
Go on with your airs, you creators of hates,
Eat well, while the dishwasher spits on the plates;
But while at your feast let the orchestra play
The life-giving strains of the dear Marseillaise,
That red revolution be placed on the throne
Till those who produce have come into their own.

But scorn me tonight, on the morn you shall learn
That those whom you loathe can despise you in turn,
The dishwasher vows that his fellows shall know
That only their ignorance keeps them below.
Your music was potent, your music hath charms,
It hardened the muscles that strengthen my arms.
It painted a vision of freedom, of life—
Tomorrow I strive for an ending of strife.

After this rendition, I was walking up the side of the hall
when I met my friend Ben Larsen. At his side was a young
girl I had never seen before, but I could not take my eyes
off her. When Ben introduced her as his sister I was glad,
because I reasoned I could keep track of Miss Muriel Larsen,
and I knew from the first moment I saw her that I never
wanted to lose sight of her.

I was no ladies' man, and it had never occurred to me that
I could fall so easily, but I never from that moment had to
think about it. I knew I wanted then and there to put my arms

77

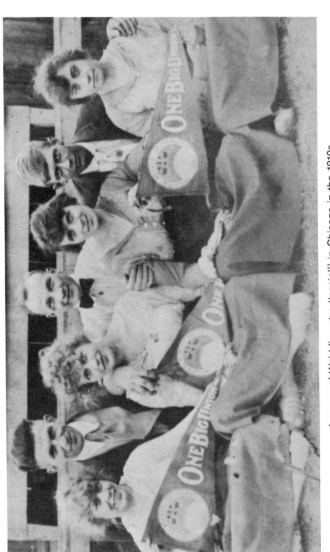

A group of Wobblies at a "social" in Chicago in the 1910s. Second from left in the front is Muriel Larson.

around her and never let her go. I was happy and scared all at the same time. Would she like me? Could I see her again? How fast those things can go round in your head!

She did see me again—in fact, the very next day, and there began a sweetness in my life I had never before known and I shall always remember. Muriel was to help me in most of my street meetings in Chicago where she sold literature and pamphlets.

A few weeks after meeting Muriel, I was called to IWW headquarters, and Bill Haywood asked me if I would go to Red Granite, Wisconsin, where there was a strike going on. I left at once, after letting Muriel know.

Arriving in Red Granite, I was met by some Italian workers and escorted to the hall where the strikers held their meetings. They were completely unorganized. I had them issue a call for a general mass meeting of all strikers from Red Granite and the adjoining town for that afternoon. When they had filled the hall, about six hundred men, I began first by having them organize a strike committee with two alternate members for each member of the committee. This was in case the police tried to arrest the whole strike committee. The committee consisted of fifteen members, and all matters of importance coming before the strike committee had first to be approved by the strikers as a whole before any agreement could be made with the bosses. Then a set of demands was drawn up in writing and the strike committee was instructed to present them to the bosses. In two days this local had a membership of over five hundred and a charter which covered both towns.

I stayed in town with an Italian family, helping where I could, but by and large letting them do most of their own work so as to leave a local with some ability to carry on its own affairs. On only one occasion did I interfere. This was when two large companies wanted to settle with the strikers independently. I thought it looked like a trap, and when I saw the members wavering a little in favor of settlement, I took the floor. I said about half of them worked for these two companies. If they accepted the proposition, half would be breaking the strike for the other half. If the bosses were sincere, they would meet the demands completely down the line. The bosses started up the aisles for me. I never saw men so mad. The strikers stopped them before they reached me, but from then on I was never left alone. At least four strikers went everywhere I did. When they had things well in hand again and there seemed to be no further need of my remaining there, I left and returned to Chicago.

I was anxious to get back. I couldn't get that girl out of my mind. I just had to see her again. I did, and spent several weeks in Chicago speaking nightly on corners and at hall meetings. Then came the news of the strike on the Mesabi Range, the iron-miners in northern Minnesota.

I was sent at once to Duluth, Minnesota, by Haywood. When I arrived in Duluth, I was elected secretary of the Duluth branch of Local 400. I was also active speaking on streetcorners, and in starting the paper which later became the mouthpiece of the strikers, the *Strikers' News*.

One day while standing in front of the IWW hall I spit, as people will do, on the sidewalk. The plainclothesmen came up to me and said I was under arrest. I asked, "What in hell for?"

"Spitting on the sidewalk," they said.

I couldn't help laughing. I told them, "Christ, you fellows are sure hard up to make a pinch."

But it did no good. They took me in and I was released on twenty-five dollars bail.

Another time I went into the office of the Duluth *Tribune* and gave the editor five or six pamphlets. I told him since he was always writing about the IWW I thought I'd do him a favor and give him something to read so he'd know what he was talking about. I stepped out of the building and there were the same two cops.

"Hello, Mac," they said.

I didn't answer.

"You're under arrest," said one.

"What did you cook up this time?"

"Inciting to riot, indecent language and abuse of the editor of the *Tribune*."

There had not been a loud word spoken. In fact, the editor had thanked me for the pamphlets, but some young reporter had phoned the cops that I was there. Well, I had to have fifty dollars put up this time. Later, a jury laughed this case out of court. The spitting case was also thrown out, but later when I and another fellow worker had gone into a saloon for a glass of beer, a fellow we had never seen before started to abuse both of us and the IWW, stating that we should all be taken out and shot, and soon. I told him to shut up, and he took a poke at me. I swung at him and landed flush on his nose. It bled all over the place. I had some on my hand when we went out of the place, and who in hell was standing right outside the door? The same two cops. They saw the blood on my hand and went inside. I learned later that they made the fellow prefer charges of assault against me. Of course they pinched me; then I was tried before a judge. One of the cops said he was in the place and saw me attack the fellow. I called him a goddamn liar right there, and for this—and not for the assault charge—I was given thirty days. I was released on fifty dollars bail, pending appeal. Later I had to make a six-hundred-mile trip back to Duluth to have this bail released to the worker who had put it up, and serve the thirty days.

The strike on the range lasted several months; however, I was released from my secretary job about the second month and Whitey Kline took over. I was called to Chicago where I made a report and had a few wonderful days with Muriel. Then I was again sent back to the Mesabi Range, this time accompanied by Richard Frazer. We went strraight through to Virginia City, Minnesota, which was the central point of the strike.

As we left the train we were at once arrested by about five Virginia City plain clothesmen. They took us to the city jail and there they threatened us with everything they could think of if we did not leave town. They pushed us around quite a bit. One would get behind us and sock us on the ribs. Then another would shove us off balance and another would shove us back. I guess they did not want to mark us up, because after quite a bit of this they said we could go, but that was just a sample of what we would get if we didn't get out of town.

But they didn't molest us again. After covering the towns on the Mesabi Range, I again went to Duluth, where I was active for a few weeks. Then I returned to Chicago where I called up Muriel and found a coldness I did not expect. I saw Muriel, and she told me it was all over. No, there was no one else. Just that it was best for the movement, or some such thing. I was in a daze for days after this; I didn't give a damn what happened.

I made my way back to Duluth where I served out the thirty days. The war in Europe was going on now and getting hotter and hotter with each day. Our meetings on streetcorners were getting more and more interruptions from all sides. It was hard sometimes to keep a free-for-all from breaking out.

It was during this time that a "Preparedness Day" parade took place and passed in front of the IWW hall in Duluth. I was standing at the door of the hall when five or six young fellows went inside. I was at once troubled with a feeling that something was in the wind. I went into the hall and, going to the back, I called a few fellow workers over and said, "Back me up!" I shouted, "Out! All out! We're going to close up the hall." The young fellows looked sort of bewildered, and one of them said, "I just want to stay awhile and read some of these booklets."

I said, "Out! Right now!"

They were no doubt waiting for a signal of some sort. We rushed them out, and I told the secretary to lock up. He said they might break the doors and windows. I asked him what the hell he cared. At least no one would get killed. The parade went past, and the young fellows left. Without any band music or crowd, they lost their courage.

Shortly after this I went to Chicago and attended a meeting at which Gurley Flynn spoke. During this meeting, while Flynn was speaking, I noticed a bulge in a fellow named Mac-Donald's overcoat pocket. I slowly reached over and, little by little, I pulled out a Chicago police blackjack. Just as I got it out of his pocket, he felt it and turned. I handed the blackjack to someone else behind me, and where it went I never knew. Ralph Chaplin was seated right behind me and saw the whole thing. After the meeting as I left the hall, I was at once pinched by two plainclothesmen. Chaplin, seeing me in trouble, came charging in to help. As he got near, he was grabbed by four cops. We were both taken to the can. Chaplin was bailed out almost at once. I was left overnight. In the morning, the judge threw the case out of court. This was how we got conclusive proof that MacDonald was a stool pigeon. While we had suspected it before, we now had real proof. He wasn't alone.

As time went on and the war got hotter and hotter and it looked more and more like the U.S. would get into it, I began to notice new faces in the IWW halls. Talk began of the kind that could only mean an attempt was being made to discredit old-timers, men who had been in the thick of things and had proven themselves. Whispers, little things which were no part of a person's loyalty to the IWW, began to appear as major crimes. It was hard to put your finger on what was happening, but we began to uncover the finks a few at a time. MacDonald in Chicago, Leiberman in Duluth, and others. There were Pinkerton men as well as government secret service men, and they were past masters of divide and rule. Old-timers began to look at each other with suspicion. Men turned up missing and were never heard from again. But for the timely interference by Jack Law, I would not be writing this. While I was walking down a railroad track with twenty or thirty other Wobblies, there were three or four in the group who were going to murder me and throw me off a high bridge. Law heard of the plot and went to the members and told them they were wrong and talked them out of it. I don't know to this day what I was going to be bumped off for.

* * *

It was about this time that we learned of the murder of Wobbly organizer Frank Little in Butte, Montana.

Butte was a mining town, a city of widows and cemeteries. At one time there were more miners buried in Butte cemeteries than were living in the city itself. Most had died of miners' consumption, lead poisoning, or fires that frequently raged in these deepest of all mines, where the normal temperature ranged between 110 and 120 degrees.

In Butte on June 18, 1917, there occurred a fire that shocked the nation. Nearly two hundred miners burned to death in the Speculator Mine. It was proven that the company had violated state mining safety laws by building solid concrete bulkheads between passages in the mine without providing man-holes between them. When the fire broke out, miners swarmed to lower levels looking for exits into other passageways. The solid bulkheads prevented them from getting through, and they were burned like rats in a trap. No mine owners were ever prosecuted for the deaths.

A few days after the fire, Butte miners went on strike for higher safety standards. Frank Little arrived on the scene in July.

Frank was a half-breed Indian, a small man, crippled, with only one good eye. I knew him well, having traveled many hundreds of miles with him on freights across the midwest. He was one of the best of the Wobs, dedicated and absolutely fearless.

On the night of July 31, 1917, he hobbled on his crutch to the cheap rooming-house where he was staying and went to bed. Sometime during the night, six men entered his room, tied him up and took him outside where they hitched him to the rear of their car. They dragged him face down out of town.

He was found hanging to a railroad trestle the next morning—beaten, desexed, his kneecaps dragged off before they killed him. Pinned to his underwear was a note, "Others take notice! First and last warning!" Other organizers in Butte later received copies of the same warning. Frank's murderers were never caught or even seriously sought by the Butte power structure they had served so well.

In the late summer of 1917, Nef sent me to Burdette, Minnesota, where I was to organize and collect dues in the logging country. It was as much as your life was worth to let it be known you were an IWW organizer, and no one would even talk to me, let alone admit they were members. Burdette got pretty tough. It was here that I learned of the simultaneous government raids on Wobbly halls and headquarters all over the country, and of the Federal indictment against top Wobbly leaders. I was among them. We were charged with "conspiracy to obstruct the war effort." Our real crime was fighting for a better, richer life for the working class.

Being known in Burdette, I left town at night and went to a little place called Warroad at the extreme north of Minnesota. I remained there all summer working on the lake with a fishing company, and then ran a skating rink in the winter, when I came close to starving to death for lack of business.

I made a trip to Red Lake Falls and was there only a few hours trying to look up some IWW members, when I got in a beef with a logger and was thrown in the can. Next morning, I gave the judge a check for ten dollars on a Warroad bank, explaining I did not have it in the bank, but would put it in as soon as I got to Warroad. I don't know what he ever did with that check. I know I never made it good.

A fellow in Warroad, a storekeeper, had begun to get ideas about me and was always asking me questions.I knew it would only be a matter of time until I was arrested, so I took off and hiked out of Warroad.

I hired out to a backwoods rancher to cut railroad ties at twenty-five cents a piece. I worked until I had enough to pay my fare as far as Madison, Wisconsin, where I found a job in a restaurant. I followed the course of what was happening to the Wobblies who had surrendered or been picked up by watching the papers. When I found out that they had let themselves be talked into being tried together instead of each demanding a jury trial, I decided it was not for me. Whoever talked them into this course of action I do not know. I do know, however, that it was the worst thing they could have done. If they had demanded separate jury trials, they never could have tried them all, and I am sure the war would have been over before they got halfway through. I thought at times of giving myself up, but to pose like a sitting duck with a hundred of my fellow workers, waiting for old Judge Kenesaw Mountain Landis to lower the boom—this I could not do.

To have a chance to defend myself before a jury, being tried alone on whatever charges they brought before the court—this chance, for myself and my fellow workers, I would have taken. But to fall into the trap it turned out to be was not for me. What Mountain Landis did to the Wobs on trial there in Chicago is a matter of history. This "friendly Man." as they thought, meted out 5, 10, and 20 years like he was punishing hardened criminals. His reward for beginning the official persecution of the Wobblies, and the destruction of the IWW as a significant movement, was $100,000 a year as Commissioner of Baseball.

I decided against prison and returned to Paterson, New Jersey, where I was voluntarily inducted into the Army. My life there was like that of thousands of others like me, so I won't dwell on it here. When I was discharged at the end of 1919 I went back home to Paterson where, while selling Christmas trees on a main corner, I was approached by a former Wobbly whom I recognized. We talked a long time and then I asked him, "Do you know what became of Muriel Larsen, or where she is?" He told me she had worked for IWW headquarters at Chicago until the government raids, and a letter there might contact her. I wrote the letter and after some time had passed, received a reply.

I don't know how to explain my feelings at this time. When Muriel wrote me, I only know that somehow something that had been lost for a long time had been found again. She kept me from going at once to South Dakota where she was teaching school. We corresponded for some time and became engaged. By then I was working for the Erie Railroad, and I asked for a pass and went to Chicago to meet Muriel. We were married there, and from here on is a story which is not mine to tell; it belongs to both of us, but mostly to my wife, pal, and the mother of our five children.

As I look back now, I guess I'm proud of this: that I worked for a better world for people to live in and did my part within the structure of an organization I was sure had the answers, and for that day and time, it did. But I am not lulled into any belief that ours was a group of men who were beyond reproach. There were times when to take an opposing view from that of the top leadership would not only put you out of activity, but might just as easily end you up along a railroad right-of-way with your brains bashed in. We had some self-styled saviors of the working class who had murder in their hearts. What happened to W.T. Nef, a real hero of the movement, both in and out of jail, isn't a pretty story, I know. But by and large, we were decent men and women who fought the day to day battles, took the blows, and shed the blood that made today's labor movement possible, a movement that could profit from a fresh infusion of Wobbly commitment to social justice.

We made mistakes, but were destroyed as an organization only because we were too successful. We made our mark.

"Thrown on the Scrap Heap"—a photograph by Saffo, reproduced in the *International Socialist Review*, illustrating Henry McGuckin's article, "An Old-Timer"

AN OLD-TIMER

When the Home Guard worker is thrown on the industrial scrap heap he is, at least, surrounded by friends and relatives. He has been a resident of the town and is well known in the community. Through the influence of some of his friends he can get into the County Poor House. But far different is the story of the migratory worker.

On account of the industrial conditions, the migratory worker is forced from place to place in search of a job. A few weeks' work in the harvest fields, and then he is off to some construction job which is completed perhaps in two or three months, making it impossible for the migratory worker to have a home.

He cannot vote at the city election; he has no political pull; he has no influential friends; no bank account. He belongs to no church or lodge. It is true that he pays hospital fees every month whenever he is employed, but the moment he leaves the job his receipt for hospital fee is null and void. Sometimes he has two or three jobs in a month.

In Humboldt County, California, the labor unions maintain one of the best equipped hospitals on the Pacific Coast. For ten dollars a year a worker can get a Union Labor Hospital ticket.

But the lumber corporations still collect the monthly hospital fee, in spite of the fact that many of the men are paying into their own hospital.

The trade unions of Eureka, California, took this case to the Supreme Court of the state. What did the Supreme Court decide? It maintained that the employer could not take out the hospital fee against the will of the employee, but the employer can, upon employing a man, lay down certain regulations and conditions, and if the employee does not care to accept them the employer can refuse him employment.

According to the Supreme Court, it is unlawful for the boss to do this, but if the slave does not like it he can become a tramp. Such is the way of the law.

The following is the story of one Jack O'Brien, one of the many thousands of worn-out migratory workers.

In the summer of 1912 the Modesto Water Company was constructing an irrigation canal near Modesto, California. Through the fault of the company-loving foreman's attempts to save powder, a certain blast did not do its work, leaving an overhanging ledge of dirt and rock. Some of the workmen protested, saying the cut was dangerous. But the foreman commanded them to get back on the job.

Contrary to the opinion of our well-to-do and comfortable "public" that the hobo will not work, the men realized that if they refused to go on they would again be thrown out of work on an already overcrowded labor market to become tramps, facing the hardships of hunger and want, and they struck.

We met O'Brien at Colfax, California, huddled up to a campfire with a few blankets and some tin cans between some bushes, and a canvas stretched out overhead. This was his home. O'Brien is sixty-five years old. He was injured making profits for a boss. The Marshal of Colfax refused to send him to the County Hospital. The trainmen refused to give him a lift. With a crippled foot and the rheumatism, he is unable to walk. The only food he gets is from passing hoboes or migratory workers. This is very little, for these men have not much for themselves.

What about the California Compensation Act? Well, O'Brien was hurt before this act became a law. And even if he had been hurt after, it is doubtful if he would have benefited.

And so there he lies on the Scrap Heap, worn out and lonely, awaiting the appearance of the passing hobo who may be kind enough and sufficiently supplied to stop and cook up a meal which he may share.

Like a worn-out machine that can no longer be used, O'Brien lies rejected of respectable society. This is the story of the migratory worker and every worker everywhere today.

Ye slaves, arise! The remedy for such conditions lies in organization. Unite in One Big Union and build up a system of society wherein every worker will be able to live like a human being. Then when our Day of Work is done, we shall know that a comfortable old age awaits us. The man who has planted and harvested shall spend his days in plenty. The builder shall have a roof over his head. And comfort shall be his portion. The man who has toiled shall not want for any needful thing! Then men like poor old Jack O'Brien will have something to look forward to besides a six-foot plot of ground, a barrel of quicklime and the Potter's Field.

Henry McGuckin

International Socialist Review
August 1914

AFTERWORD

Mac and Muriel, my father and mother, were married in May, 1920. They remained committed radicals and paid the requisite dues for their convictions and activities all their lives. Shortly after their marriage, for example, they barely escaped an armed mob of American Legionnaires while on an organizing drive in Georgia for the radical American Veterans' Committee. During the 1930s they were fired and blacklisted in the California Napa valley for organizing the state's largest "Progressive Club" among poor farmers, workers, and residents of the local veterans' hospital where Mac was a federal employee in charge of the kitchens. The audacity of the club in running Mac for the State Assembly on the "Farmer-Labor" ticket stirred the local Chamber of Commerce into action and, with a little help from General George Marshall (who flew to California for the purpose), federal rules were circumvented and Mac was fired. Muriel lost her job as Napa city hall librarian, and my teen-aged elder brother was fired as manager of the local Postal Telegraph office where he had worked his way up from messenger boy. With no work in the area for any McGuckin, Mac and Muriel packed up and moved on, which pretty much describes the pattern of their lives.

Their personal lives, too, were characterized by constant struggle. When not blacklisted, Mac could usually find work somehow, but periodic, losing battles with alcohol sometimes cost him those he didn't lose for political reasons. And in her mid-thirties, Muriel suffered a sudden paralysis of her legs and the slower loss of her sight from a never fully understood disease of the spinal cord.

But political repression and personal tragedy notwithstanding, in my childhood memories the McGuckin household rings with song—Muriel, blind, in her wheelchair at an old upright piano singing Joe Hill's verses in her lusty, lilting soprano, with Mac's mellow baritone in support, while their five children distributed varied harmonies as best they could. And I remember the roar of argument as old Wobs, Communists, Trotskyists, Anarchists, Equalitarian Socialists, et al., gathered at Mac and Muriel's for radical communion and sometimes, to reminisce. (How fascinating to a child were those wonderful stories told around the table by those who had lived them, stories of strikes and jail, soap boxes and free-speech fights, heroes, heroines and martyrs.)

Mac and Muriel lived most of their lives at the edge of poverty or over it, but the richness of their political commitments was more than adequate compensation; their politics gave meaning to their lives and comprised their proud gift to their children. We were never permitted to forget our radical heritage, and it was expected that each of us would filter the peculiar qualities of our particular generational experiences through the cleansing sieve of our "background." (I remember, at fifteen, setting off to a public tennis court with a second-hand, broken-stringed racket to my mother's plaintive query, "But, Mick, isn't tennis a *bourgeois* sport?")

Muriel's physical ailments eventually overcame even her indomitable good spirits as pain and bed-ridden total dependence stripped her of that minimum of personal dignity she demanded. In 1963, she instructed Mac, her children, and her doctor of her intentions and chose euthanasia, the "good death," as we all gathered around her bed to be with her and to ward off, literally, the interference of the state.

In the years immediately following Muriel's death, Mac lived alone near his children. He shared in the resurgence of interest in the Wobblies during the 1960s, was occasionally invited to address radical student groups in Berkeley and San Francisco, was honored guest at a variety of social-political affairs, and once shared with Cesar Chavez Wobbly experiences and strategies for organizing migratory workers.

It was during this period that I asked my father to record his experiences as a Wobbly. To his protests of his inablity to write grammatically, I responded with the suggestion that he simply write the way he talked. He did, and these *Memoirs* are the result. My task as his editor was light, for this work is my father's authentic voice, the way he spoke when he told those stories which so facinated me as a child. And still do.

In 1974, aged eighty, weakened by severe emphysema and losing the mobility to live alone and independently, Mac addressed a farewell to family, friends and fellow workers, flung a final curse at "the lies and rottenness of the whole damn system," and took Muriel's path.

Mac and Muriel left five children, eleven grandchildren, and eight great grandchildren the legacy of their examples: they recognized the barricades in every form; they knew which side they must be on; they found the courage to be there.

H. E. McGuckin Jr., Ph.D.
San Francisco State University